Three sad races
Racial identity and national consciousness in Brazilian literature

Three sad races

Racial identity and national consciousness
in Brazilian literature

David T. Haberly

Department of Spanish, Italian and Portuguese
University of Virginia

Cambridge University Press

Cambridge
London   New York   New Rochelle
Melbourne   Sydney

Published by the Press Syndicate of the University of Cambridge
The Pitt Building, Trumpington Street, Cambridge CB2 1RP
32 East 57th Street, New York, NY 10022, USA
296 Beaconsfield Parade, Middle Park, Melbourne 3206, Australia

First published 1983

Printed in the United States of America

Library of Congress Cataloging in Publication Data
Haberly, David T.
Three sad races.
Bibliography: p.
Includes index.
1. Brazilian literature – History and
criticism.   2. Nationalism and literature –
Brazil.   3. Race awareness in literature.
I. Title.
PQ9522.N27H3   869'.09'981   82-4467
ISBN 0 521 24722 5   AACR2

The author wishes to thank the following for supplying the photographs that appear on chapter-opening pages: Editôra Nova Aguilar (Antônio Gonçalves Dias and Antônio de Castro Alves), *Manchete* (José de Alencar and João da Cruz e Sousa), Biblioteca Nacional de Rio de Janeiro (Joaquim Maria Machado de Assis), and João Cândido Portnari (photograph of the portrait of Mário de Andrade by his father, Cândido Portinari).

TO CAROL

WHO TAUGHT ME HOW TO WRITE

Contents

Acknowledgments

This book owes a great deal to a number of people and institutions. I am grateful, first, to two of my teachers, Francis M. Rogers and Raymond S. Sayers. I am also grateful to friends and colleagues, in Brazil and the United States, for their assistance and encouragement: Haroldo de Campos, Kenneth Chastain, Nereu Corrêa, Santiago Daydí-Tolson, João David Ferreira Lima, David Gies, Javier Herrero, Lemuel Johnson, Rosa Konder, Roberto and Magda Laus, Alfred Mac Adam, Jane Malinoff, Thomas Skidmore, and Jon Tolman. Any errors of fact or interpretation, of course, are entirely my own.

The Interlibrary Loan Office of the University of Virginia library tracked down an astonishing number of rare and obscure publications for me. My research in Brazil was greatly facilitated by the staffs of the libraries of the federal universities of Ceará and Santa Catarina; the municipal libraries of Florianópolis, Fortaleza, and São Paulo; the National Library in Rio; and the collection of the Brazilian Academy of Letters. My two research trips to Brazil were made possible by the Virginia–Santa Catarina partnership of the Partners of the Americas and by the University of Virginia, which awarded me a Sesquicentennial Research Associateship.

Very special thanks go to my wife, whose invaluable assistance proved once again how handy it is to have a professional writer and editor around the house.

All translations in the text, unless otherwise noted, are my own; the Portuguese originals of individual poems cited in English translation can be found in the notes.

Brazilian poetry frequently uses ellipsis (*reticências*) as a literary device; this usage is shown, in the translations, by unspaced periods. The standard English ellipsis, signifying the omission of portions of a cited text, appears as spaced periods.

D. T. H.

Introduction

The Brazilian poet Olavo Bilac declared, in the second decade of the twentieth century, that the music of his nation was the "loving flower of three sad races" (*"flor amorosa de três raças tristes"*) (1964:263). Bilac was in many ways the epitome of *fin de siècle* Brazil – diligently superficial in his literary creations and in his cultural judgments, fervently if fuzzily patriotic, and resoundingly bourgeois in his attitudes toward art and society. His dictum was hardly the product of a radical consciousness, and it was widely accepted by his contemporaries as both deeply poetic and profoundly true. Most Brazilians, then and now, would unhesitatingly extend it to describe the nation's literature as well as its music.

Two discrete concepts coexist in Bilac's summation of this national consensus: the multiracial nature of Brazilian culture, and the sadness inherent in the national soul. The Portuguese, in Bilac's interpretation of Brazil's musical – and cultural – history, sang songs filled with nostalgia for the homeland they had left behind. The Indians joined in to mourn the world the white man had taken from them. The Africans, brought to Brazil in chains, wept for the freedom they had lost.

But Bilac was not referring simply to the first decades of Brazilian history, for the theme of national sadness – an existential sense of suffering, of exile, and of loss – survived the assimilation of the Portuguese, the virtual disappearance of the Indian, and the abolition of African slavery; by Bilac's day, it was deeply embedded in the consciousness of the independent Republic. One decade later, in 1928, Paulo Prado suggested that this sad-

1

ness was fundamental to the national character, subtitling his *Portrait of Brazil* (*Retrato do Brasil*) *An Essay on the Sadness of Brazil.* The idea that Brazil – and Brazilian literature – is the end result of the interaction of these three racial groups is even more of a commonplace in the national consciousness than this conviction of sadness. It must be admitted, moreover, that the idea is firmly based, at least for literature, upon reality: Of the six major figures studied in this volume, four are nonwhite.

The multiracial character of Brazilian literary history, however, goes far beyond genetics. As we shall see, much of Brazil's literature has been preoccupied with an anguished search for a viable racial identity – a search that has been both personal and national in scope. In this endeavor, Bilac's two themes of race and of suffering have been joined again and again; the most emotional example, perhaps, is Guilherme de Almeida's 1925 description of the nation as a "cross in whose shadow / three races crossed and mixed, three different bloods dripped from three crucified victims" (1952:191).

This Brazilian tradition is particularly striking when set against the generally optimistic North American belief in the inherent viability and perfectibility of social and cultural institutions. And, despite the essential similarity of the racial backgrounds of the United States and Brazil, Americans have illogically but decisively defined themselves and their nation in terms of the white majority alone. American literature, with pitifully few exceptions, has been written by whites, for whites, and about whites. Nonwhite characters have been marginal at best, serving only to highlight the white heroes or heroines, the only conceivable national symbols.

The gap between this American tradition of whiteness and optimism and Guilherme de Almeida's tortured vision of three victims of different colors is the result of contrasting definitions of the nature of race and of the function of literature. In the United States, racial identity has been simply and clearly defined as almost entirely a question of genetics. Although there is some evidence that this ancestry-based system of racial classification has been applied to Indians and to other minorities, its operation can best be understood in its application to black Americans.[1] A black, in the American tradition, is a person with at least one African ancestor – however convoluted the family tree.[2] The genetic basis of racial categories in the United States can be clearly seen in American English: The term "mulatto" has traditionally been applied to individuals with one white and one black parent; the now obsolete "quadroon" (one black grandparent) and "octoroon" (one black great-grandparent) were even more mathematically precise.

The far more complex Brazilian system operates in a very different way, but a system of racial categories, equally founded upon prejudice toward nonwhite peoples, does exist.[3] Briefly stated, this system functions on several distinct but closely interconnected levels. Simple genetic ancestry, the single focus of the North American system, is but one level. Equally important in Brazil are physical characteristics associated with race – skin pigmentation, hair color and texture, and the contours of the nose and lips – and such cultural patterns as dress, religion, education, and speech. All three levels – ancestry, somatology, and culture – form a continuum, founded upon prejudice-based value judgments, that ranges from African or Indian to European, from ugliness to beauty, from barbarism to civilization.

The racial identity of any individual – his or her position on the continuum – is not necessarily fixed and immutable, as it so often is in the United States, but is constantly redefined by the perceptions of others, perceptions that can vary greatly from region to region and within different social settings. As an American sociologist sums up the system, race is in the eye of the beholder:

Socially, color or race is a continuum running from black to white and so perceived by members of Brazilian society and, while the continuum is firmly anchored at either extreme, the intermediate categories are flexible in that they are variously defined by different persons and may be variously applied by different persons to the same person. Thus, evaluation of color in the intermediate categories is partly idiosyncratic and personal. [Saunders, 1972:144]

Each Brazilian, therefore, whatever his own feelings about the reality of his racial background, daily presents himself for careful inspection and classification by those he meets. And even the elite, very sure of its own whiteness, has tended to view the national population as a whole as nonwhite and, therefore, inferior.

This conviction of national inferiority does not depend upon statistics (the very subjectivity of racial categories in Brazil makes census figures on race highly unreliable) but upon perception and, ironically, upon the elite's need to justify its own privileged position.[4] If one group within Brazil is to define itself as genetically, somatically, and culturally superior, it must believe implicitly in the inferiority – that is, the nonwhiteness – of most of the rest of the population. And yet this justification of superior status, however comforting in personal terms, has had profoundly negative effects upon the Brazilian elite's vision of the nation and its future possibilities, a vision clouded by feelings of pessimism, of frustration, of alienation. For the elite, Almeida's Calvary expressed the reality of this vision: The Indians and Africans have been tortured by whites, but are also crucified by their own inferiority; and the whites themselves are tormented by the knowledge that they are condemned to share their land with beings viewed as hopelessly and permanently inferior.

Within the context of this interplay of individual pride and national despair, literature has had a very special function for the Brazilian elite, a function that is quite alien to the American conception of the purpose and nature of literary activity. The goal of the white literature of white America has been to reach as many of the nation's readers as possible, to create a broad-based national culture, to elevate the level of that culture, and – not entirely incidentally – to sell a great many books.

Literature in Brazil, on the other hand, has been almost exclusively the creature of the elite. The proportion of the Brazilian population classified as minimally literate has not changed greatly over the last half-century, and the proportion of Brazilians who are active consumers of literature – the cultural elite of the nation – probably remained constant, from 1822 to at least 1950, at less than 1 percent.[5] As Brazilian society is structured, more-over, this cultural elite, set apart by education and inclination, as well as by the financial ability to purchase books, is also the political, social, and economic elite of the nation. And the very act of reading a literary work, for upper-class Brazilians, is there-fore an act of social self-affirmation, since that action and the abilities it presupposes are proof of membership in the elite.

The consumption of literature is not merely a ritual of class distinction, however, but a declaration of whiteness as well: The education and intelligence required to read a work of literature, after all, are part of the prejudice-based cultural and genetic definitions of race. And nonwhites who somehow manage to become consumers of literature thereby whiten themselves, in their own eyes and in the eyes of others; this phenomenon is an integral part of the process Carl Degler has called "the mulatto escape-hatch" (1971:224–5).

A further peculiarity of the Brazilian literary tradition is its narrow circularity: Those who consume literature are, to a sur-prising extent, its producers as well. The classic example of this identity of producers and consumers is Tobias Barreto, a non-white intellectual from Pernambuco, who wrote and published an erudite and highly specialized philosophical journal in Ger-man; Barreto was also almost the only Brazilian reader capable of wading through this esoteric publication. What might appear to us an absurd exercise in futility, however, was for Barreto a vital affirmation of cultural whiteness, concrete proof of his in-tellectual and social superiority. Although Barreto's case is clearly an exaggeration, it does symbolize the ritualistic nature of litera-ture in Brazil. The creation of a literary text is an act even more refined, even more aristocratic, even more whitening than the consumption of literature, and most consumers of Brazilian lit-erature have attempted seriously, generally during adolescence, to perform this highest ritual of social and racial self-affirmation.

Because, once again, the cultural and genetic components of the racial continuum define intelligence, literary ability, and educa-tion as inherently white traits, nonwhites who produce texts of merit have some real possibility of moving themselves along the continuum toward the escape hatch of perceived whiteness. In the case of the great mulatto novelist Machado de Assis, for example, some of his white contemporaries appear to have been fully persuaded, by his talent and culture, that he was literally white.

In less extreme cases, however, we do find a general tolerance of nonwhite writers of talent, at least before about 1900. Recognition of the progress of such writers along the racial continuum, after all, in no way negated the harsh and instinctive prejudice that is as much the basis of race relations in Brazil as it is in the United States; the achievements of those of mixed blood could always, in the final analysis, be explained away as the triumph of white genes over African or Indian genes. This system, in fact, was severely tested only once in nineteenth-century Brazil, in the case of João da Cruz e Sousa, a figure whose racial origins and appearance placed him irrevocably at the extreme black end of the continuum.

The creation of literature, however, is more than merely a ritualistic declaration of whiteness and elite status. As I have suggested, most educated Brazilians have traditionally endeavored to produce literary works – primarily poetry – during adolescence. Such efforts are seen as entirely natural, as well as laudable, because of the almost universal conviction that although literature may presuppose inborn talent and a vocation, it is above all the result of some sort of creative crisis, a by-product of the kind of suffering, marginality, and alienation considered typical of the passage from youth to maturity. The creative crisis, though most common during adolescence, may nonetheless occur at any stage in life. Old José Bonifácio de Andrada e Silva, the "Patriarch of Brazilian Independence" and as tough a political in-fighter as the nation's history has seen, published a little book of poems while exiled from the land he had helped make free. Exile also moved Dom Pedro II – emperor of Brazil from 1841 to 1889 – to turn his hand to verse (1898).

This, then, is the ultimate irony of Brazilian literature: Literary creativity is public proof of genetic and social superiority; it is also, simultaneously, the result of a private crisis of misery and alienation. By logical extension, great texts presuppose uncommon suffering. The idealized, even sentimentalized, image of the tragic writer was a Romantic commonplace throughout Western culture; Brazilian literature of the nineteenth century had more than its share of brilliant young poets who suffered greatly – or who convinced themselves that they suffered greatly – and who died in their late teens or early twenties. The tradition of the creative crisis of sorrow and exile, however, can be traced back to the seventeenth century in Brazil, and has survived into our own time.

This tradition helps explain Brazilian acceptance of a handful of nonwhite writers as central figures in the nation's literature. If one accepts the hypothesis that literary creativity derives from suffering and alienation, and if one also accepts Brazilian ideas and expectations about race, it is only reasonable to conclude that nonwhiteness itself can be viewed as a supreme creative crisis of physical misery, psychological exile, and social marginality.

The relationship I have noted between literature and the relatively brief creative crisis of adolescence, and between literary achievement and the far more profound and enduring creative crisis of nowhiteness itself, not only serves to define the origins and nature of the production of individual writers, but also, by extension, determines the character and the purpose of Brazilian literature as a whole. Brazilians have always tended, even in this century, to look at their nation and its culture in terms of the model of human psychological and physical development, defining Brazil itself as an adolescent – weaned from Portuguese colonialism, but still dependent upon external influences and not yet ready to stand alone as an adult member of the family of nations.

Critical to this self-definition of Brazil as an adolescent is the widespread recognition of the lack of a clear-cut, fully accepted racial and national identity, and the complementary conviction that such a single, unifying identity can and must be found. This conviction has been particularly intense in Brazil precisely because the culture that gave birth to the nation, that of Portugal, has appeared to possess just such an identity, forged by the Reconquest and by maritime expansion. A single text, the *Lusiads* of Luís de Camões – the product of the poet's long exile from Portugal – has seemed to Brazilians to provide Portugal with a supreme national text, an act of self-definition that has both expressed and reinforced that vital unity and identity.

The Portuguese identity, however comforting to white Brazilians, has generally been rejected since the early years of the nineteenth century as part of the colonial childhood of the nation; its loss is a major factor in the sadness and frustration of the Brazilian elite. The lack of the sort of coherent and cohesive self-image Brazilians attribute to Portugal has been a major factor, moreover, in the definition of Brazil and its culture as adolescent, filled with uncertainty and self-doubt. Yet the adoption of any unifying identity that is entirely white would serve only to deny the reality of the nation. Such a self-image could not be truly Brazilian. At the same time, the racial prejudice that allows white Brazilians and those who manage to be perceived as members of the elite to justify their own superior status inevitably leads to profound disquiet about the implications of any national identity that is less than totally white.

This paradox is the crux of the creative crisis of Brazil-as-adolescent, the source of the anguish and alienation that have served to form the nation's literature. Brazil's writers, by definition themselves the victims of personal misery and marginality, have ironically been charged with a central and heroic role in the formation of a new national identity; it has been their function, and their responsibility, to fuse their own creative crises with the psychological crisis of the nation in order to present possible solutions to the paradox, to point out possible pathways to maturity and self-confidence.

This book is not intended as a literary history of Brazil. Although the authors studied are arranged in chronological order, and are linked to the schools and movements to which they belonged, any student of Brazilian literature will note that some major writers, particularly those of the twentieth century, are excluded or mentioned only in passing. My purpose, rather, is to present and analyze the solutions to the Brazilian paradox – the possible national and racial identities – that appear in the works of six of Brazil's greatest and most influential writers during the period from 1840 to 1940. All of these poets and novelists wrote *about* Brazil, but their function and their importance to the nation's literature and its readers go far beyond mere description. They also quite literally wrote Brazil itself, creating a series of very different possible Brazils, diverse images of the nation's past and future – of whites, of blacks, of Indians, and of various combinations of Bilac's "three sad races" – to be placed upon the continuum and evaluated by the perceptions and prejudices of their readers in a literary replication on a national scale of the process of examination and categorization through which the racial identity of individual Brazilians is daily defined and redefined.

1

From Indians to Indianism

When Pedro Álvares Cabral discovered Brazil for Portugal in April of 1500, his literal-minded scribe, Pêro Vaz de Caminha, was moved by the beauty of a new land and a new people to set down a poetic vision of infinite fertility and innocence. Caminha was struck, almost at first glance, by the apparently inexhaustible abundance and goodness of the land – and by the fact that what he saw appeared to serve no useful purpose (Cortesão, 1967:251).

Caminha viewed the natives of this land in the same terms – as inherently and potentially good, but desperately in need of development. The Indian men, he noted, were uncircumcised, "all just as we are" (Ley, 1947:47), and he took this as fundamental proof that Brazil's inhabitants had not been sullied by contact with the circumcised enemies of Iberian Catholicism, Moslems and Jews. "My opinion and everyone's opinion is that these people lack nothing to become completely Christian except understanding us; for they accepted as we do all they saw us do, which makes us consider that they have no idolatry or worship" (Ley, 1947:58).

This pious zeal coexisted with a strong but repressed sexuality. In Caminha's detailed descriptions of Indian women, his attention repeatedly focused on their genitals; the Portuguese word he used, *vergonhas* (literally, "shames"), sums up the conflict of cultural patterns that both perturbed and excited him. "One of those girls," he wrote, "was all colored from head to toe with that paint they use; and surely she was so well-formed and so rounded and her shameful parts (about which she felt no shame) were so comely that many women of our own land, seeing such perfection, would be ashamed that their parts were not equally perfect."[1]

One of Caminha's central themes, the lush beauty of the land, was repeated and embellished by the isolated chroniclers and poets of the early colonial period. Brazilian literary historians call this common reaction *ufanismo*: the triumphant enumeration of resources and novelties, of new plants, new animals, new landscapes. There is, however, something troubling about these hymns to the perfection of the land – an undercurrent of stridency, of anxious exaggeration, of concern that Brazil's peoples and cultures might not be worthy of such a magnificent land.

Caminha's vision of the Indian as an integral part of the beauty and purity of Brazil did survive the Portuguese conquest, preserved in the works of a few authors, primarily clerics, who still believed in the natural goodness and inherent perfectibility of the natives and who even dreamed of some fusion of the best of Amerindian and European culture. For other writers, however, the natives were but another of Brazil's innumerable curiosities, a natural resource to be aggressively exploited. The Indians' practice of cannibalism, carefully and almost erotically described by many authors, served to justify both this exploitation and the creation of a new social order based upon transplanted European culture and dominated by the Portuguese and native-born white Brazilians.

These contrasting views of colonial Brazil and its prospects appear clearly in the works of two great figures of the seventeenth century, Gregório de Matos and Father Antônio Vieira. The early optimism of *ufanismo*, however, has largely disappeared from these works. The land remains, as glorious as ever, but the presentiment of unworthiness only hinted at before has ripened into the conviction that the perfection of nature and the promise of a new society have been irremediably betrayed, by both man and God.

Gregório de Matos (1633–96), born in Brazil and educated in Portugal, bitterly assailed the mediocrity of colonial society in satirical poems that were never published, but that appear to have circulated widely in manuscript form. Like many of his readers, Gregório felt himself trapped between the ignorant arrogance of the mighty, primarily recent arrivals from Portugal, and the pretensions of those he defined as his social and racial inferiors. He was particularly disquieted by the colony's freedmen and mulattoes, sure that the Portuguese-born aristocracy gave far too much liberty and far too many privileges to beings he considered subhuman, even simian (Peres, 1967). Gregório wrote of Bahia:

> What are her favorite geegaws?...Nigras.
> And what other goods suit her needs?...Half-breeds.
> But which are her best-loved beaux?...Mulattoes.[2]

Dark-skinned women, however, were an entirely different matter for Gregório and his readers. His affection for women of his own race and station was depressingly Platonic, an excuse for metaphysical disquisitions on the mutability of emotions and the impermanence of physical beauty. Gregório satirized and chastened others who pursued *negras* and *mulatas*; for himself, however, he found it natural, even inevitable. His favorite fantasy – the immoral woman of color who cheerfully bestows her abundant favors on master, overseer, and any other able-bodied white male who happens along – was to become far and away the most popular nonwhite stereotype in Brazilian literature. This wishful image of the perpetually willing dark female, implying both the greater desirability and the superior sexuality of white males, was both a national daydream and a rationalization for a social system that openly encouraged miscegenation (Queiroz Júnior, 1975).

The sense of betrayal in the works of Father Antônio Vieira (1608–97) went far deeper than Gregório's complaints about the loss of privilege and status. Vieira's most important sermons and tracts dealt directly with his central preoccupation: the nature of God's feelings toward Portugal and its empire. The rapid expansion of the Lusitanian thalassocracy in the sixteenth century had convinced many Portuguese that they were indeed God's chosen people, charged with the discovery and conversion of new lands and peoples. Portugal's humiliating absorption into the Spanish Empire between 1580 and 1640 and the consequent loss of many of its major overseas colonies and commercial operations suggested to Vieira that the nation had fallen from divine grace. In his early "Sermon against the Arms of Holland" ("Sermão pelo Bom Sucesso das Armas de Portugal contra as da Holanda"), Vieira pugnaciously took God to task for deserting his faithful servants (Cidade, 1940:II, 157–86). A half-century later, in the bitter resignation of his "Twenty-seventh Sermon on the Rosary" ("Sermão Vigésimo Sétimo, da Série 'Maria, Rosa Mística' "), Vieira concluded that the empire had been betrayed not by a capricious deity, but by mankind's own unworthiness. All of Portugal's many political and military misfortunes throughout the world, during more than a century of captivity and defeat and failure, were necessary and well-deserved penalties imposed by God for the nation's monstrous sins of racial prejudice and exploitation, sins made manifest in Indian and African slavery in Brazil (Cidade, 1940:III, 73–114).

By the middle of the eighteenth century, the sense of betrayal so evident in the works of Vieira and Matos was temporarily drowned out by the clamorous triumph of a new *ufanismo*, based upon concrete proof that the land was truly as rich and glorious as sixteenth-century pride had maintained: Gold and diamonds were discovered in the interior. The province of Minas Gerais, the site of the first great gold rush of modern history, was at least as wild and woolly as California or the Klondike. The seemingly endless flow of precious metal and diamonds had begun to slow to a trickle by the last quarter of the eighteenth century, but economic decline scarcely altered the character of the population in that province: adventurers and prostitutes, criminals and renegade priests. Yet the great wealth of the mines and the complex demands of its administration within the colonial system had also attracted some very different inhabitants. In the capital, Vila Rica do Ouro Prêto, wrote an admittedly *ufanista* propagan-

dist in 1734, "live the chief merchants, whose trade and importance incomparably exceed the most thriving of the leading
merchants of Portugal...Here dwell the best educated men,
both lay and ecclesiastic. Here is the seat of all the nobility and
the strength of the military" (in Boxer, 1962:162–3).

Those "best educated men" included a few remarkable poets:
Tomás Antônio Gonzaga (1744–1810?), Cláudio Manuel da Costa
(1729–89), and Inácio José de Alvarenga Peixoto (1744?–93). It is
difficult, as we read the historical record of whores, smugglers,
and fugitive slaves, to imagine these highly cultured intellects
within that context – as if Thoreau or Emerson had gone out to
help run San Francisco or Dodge City. And we can sense the
appeal, for these lawyers and bureaucrats, of the artificial, imag-
inary world portrayed in the poems they wrote above all for
themselves. Literature provided an escape from the raw reality
of Brazil into the consoling vision of Arcady, a land of peace and
neatly clipped grass, of racial purity, of lovely nymphs, of handsome, freedom-loving, and deeply poetic shepherds:

> Marília, I am not some cowherd,
> Living to tend another's kine,
> Hard-bitten, coarse-mouthed features burned
> By endless suns and winter's rime.
> I have my own farm; there I dwell;
> It gives the wine, the fruit I use.
> I drink the milk of snow-white ewes
> And weave their wool to dress so well.
>   Give thanks, fair maid, with me,
>   For thus my stars decree.[3]

Reality intruded inescapably, however, in 1789, when the Portuguese authorities in Minas Gerais rounded up a motley group
of dissidents, intellectuals, soldiers, and clerics; they were charged
with conspiring to utilize the very real local discontent with
heavy taxation and bad administration as the fulcrum for active
revolt against Portugal and in favor of Brazilian independence.
Arcady could provide no refuge: Gonzaga and Alvarenga Peixoto
were convicted of participating in this abortive uprising, the

Inconfidência Mineira, and were exiled to Africa; Cláudio Manuel da Costa, awaiting trial on similar charges, was found hanged in his cell.

Ironically, Brazil's final political and cultural independence owed very little to the Arcadian poets of the Inconfidência Mineira; far more important was the memory of the Indians Caminha had seen in 1500. The Noble Savage – the native of Brazil, in many cases, as depicted by French voyagers of the sixteenth and seventeenth centuries – became a literary commonplace in eighteenth-century Europe, personifying the pure virtue of the natural man and symbolizing Romantic dreams of greater freedom. That stereotype was eventually to influence, if only to a degree, the course of events in France (Melo Franco, 1937). The French Revolution and the rise of Napoleon, in turn, led directly to the independence of Brazil and the formation of a national literature whose primary characteristic in its first decades of existence was the idealization of the Indian as the fundamental Brazilian symbol.

As Napoleon's armies threatened Lisbon, in November of 1807, the Portuguese royal family decided to lead a mass exodus – some fifteen thousand refugees in all – to the more secure lands of Brazil, the last great jewel in the battered imperial crown. João VI of Portugal ruled Brazil until he returned to Lisbon in 1821, and his presence drastically transformed the economic and cultural life of the colony: Ports were opened to trade with friendly nations; libraries and schools were founded; at long last, the first printing press was established.

João left his son Pedro in charge of a bustling and self-confident colony whose inhabitants, particularly in the capital, Rio de Janeiro, were simply not prepared to return to the stagnation and dependency of the past. Nevertheless, genuine independence was such a slow and peaceful process, developing gradually during 1821 and 1822, that historians are hard pressed to pinpoint the exact date of separation from Portugal. Brazilians celebrate 7 September 1822 – when Pedro, a flamboyant young man, cried "Independence or Death!" while riding near São Paulo –

but several other dates would do as well. Within a few months, in any case, all of Brazil had accepted independence, but it is not clear that its inhabitants felt any real involvement in the movement.

Pedro I left Brazil to seek the Portuguese crown in April of 1831; the country he had led to independence was in the hands of his infant son and a triumvirate of regents. Without the unifying symbol of a ruling monarch, the young Empire almost degenerated into a Balkan patchwork of tiny nations. This unrest was calmed only in 1840, when Pedro II – only fourteen years old – agreed to assume the crown before his majority in an attempt to unify the country. Brazil's highly intelligent and enlightened young emperor did manage to preserve territorial unity, but there was still little sense of national identity and pride.

The central institution in the intellectual search for a unifying identity was the Brazilian Historical and Geographical Institute, founded in 1838, the oldest Latin American learned society still in existence. Members of the institute turned to the colonial past for clues to the nation's present and future, but there was really very little choice. The recently expelled Portuguese were clearly unacceptable as models, as were the nation's alien and brutalized African slaves; educated Brazilians were equally unwilling to adopt the mestizo, the mulatto, or the *cafuzo* (the product of Indian and African parentage) as national symbols.

This left only the Indian, long since exterminated in most coastal areas or forced into the interior; extravagant virtues and talents could thus be imputed to this dimly remembered creature. "Indian fever" first appeared briefly during the reign of Pedro I: Portuguese surnames were replaced with Indian ones, and the emperor himself took the name of Guatimozim, the last Aztec ruler of Mexico, as his Masonic alias (Calmon, 1940:II, 20). Pedro II learned to speak Tupi, and worked on a grammar of that Indian language (Schaden and Pereira, 1969:441). Francisco Adolfo de Varnhagen, the first important historian of the new nation, urged the institute in 1840 to "ask immediately and forcefully that the government take steps to establish, in the Empire, schools in the various languages of the natives who inhabited this land and those around it" (1841:61). Varnhagen saw Tupi as a potential scientific language, useful for botany and zoology, and he also insisted that some knowledge of Indian languages would be "of great help to any writer who would devote himself to literary research for the good of the nation, feeding the spirit of nationalism, . . . since the national literature is the basic foundation upon which national independence and unity are built" (1841:59).

At almost the same time, a young aristocrat, Domingos José Gonçalves de Magalhães (1811–82), was spreading the gospel of European Romanticism in Brazil. The influential preface to Gonçalves de Magalhães' first collection of poems, *Poetic Sighs and Longings* (*Suspiros Poéticos e Saudades*), published in 1836, strongly emphasized both patriotism and exoticism (1865:9–15). The two independent currents of Romanticism and Indianism quickly became a single, all-powerful force, and Brazilian letters retreated into the past to idealize the painted and beplumed knights of the nation's own Middle Ages. A number of Indianist lyrics, epics, and novels appeared between 1840 and 1870, but many of these works were mediocre, pretentious, and pedantic. The Indianist movement would have remained no more than a fascinating footnote to the development of Brazilian literature, in fact, had it not been led by two of the greatest writers of the nineteenth century – Antônio Gonçalves Dias and José de Alencar.

2
The songs of an exile:
Antônio Gonçalves Dias

The last armed resistance to independence in all of Brazil was crushed at Caxias, a town in the northern province of Maranhão, on 1 August 1823 (Meireles, 1960:225–37). João Manuel Gonçalves Dias, a Portuguese immigrant and a leader of the loyalists in Caxias, fled to a nearby farm with his pregnant mistress, Vicência Ferreira. Their son, Antônio, born there on 10 August, was always proud of the close temporal and geographical connection between his own birth and that of the new nation, and stressed the coincidence in a short autobiographical sketch written in 1854 (in Bandeira, 1958:II, 633–4). But in this note, as in all his other published accounts of his own life, Antônio Gonçalves Dias totally ignored another symbolic coincidence – his ancestry.

Vicência Ferreira, Gonçalves Dias' mother, was probably a *cafuza* – part black, part Gê Indian (Miguel-Pereira, 1943:13–16). Since the poet's death, most Brazilian critics have pointed with pride to his descent from the "three sad races"; Gonçalves Dias himself, however, never openly linked his racial background to his Indianist verses. White Brazilians might invent Indian ancestors, but Gonçalves Dias could not take public pride in his bona fide native origins without admitting the double social stigma of illegitimacy and African descent.

Gonçalves Dias managed to achieve many of the goals he set for himself: a degree from the University of Coimbra; wealthy and influential friends, including Pedro II, in Brazil and Europe; prestigious positions in education and administration. His poems not only were immensely popular, but were highly praised by his Brazilian contemporaries and by leading Portuguese critics. Despite these successes, however, he always saw himself as an exile, an outsider – an attitude influenced by his early life and by his constant sense of inferiority.

When Gonçalves Dias was six, João Manuel abruptly dismissed Vicência and married a wealthy white girl who was openly hostile toward her illegitimate, dark-skinned stepchild. The poet was always intensely self-conscious about his nonwhiteness, the inescapable physical evidence of his ancestry. Described by a friend as no more than one and a half meters tall, Gonçalves Dias had a dark complexion, prominent cheek bones, and a slightly flattened nose (Leal, 1874:195–7). He appears, in fact, to have been convinced that much of his social success in the white world was due to his curiosity value as a kind of freak (Bandeira, 1958:II, 681).

By 1851, at the age of twenty-eight, Gonçalves Dias was an established poet, the author of three volumes of verse; he had

the security of a teaching position at the nation's finest second-
ary school and was a member of the prestigious Historical and
Geographical Institute; his friend Pedro II had made him a Cava-
lier of the Order of the Rose in December of 1849. But the poet
nevertheless continued to feel himself an outsider in the court,
and longed to return to Maranhão. He made the trip in 1851, but
it only reinforced his alienation and reminded him of his racial
origins and the inherent unworthiness he felt derived from those
origins. During this trip, he timidly proposed to the sister of a
good friend, only to be brusquely turned down as a most un-
suitable addition to a wealthy family proud of the purity of its
blood (Leal, 1874:106–7).

He fled back to Rio de Janeiro and quickly proposed to another girl, equally white and aristocratic, but afflicted with seri- ·
ous physical and psychological problems. This marriage proved
a total disaster, and Gonçalves Dias was to spend most of the
rest of his life trying to escape from it. He managed to obtain
government funds for research in Europe and remained there,
alone, from 1854 to 1858. He came back to Brazil only because he
was tremendously excited about his appointment as head of the
ethnographic section of a newly formed scientific commission
charged with exploring the almost unknown interior of northern
Brazil. The poet saw this commission as a chance to establish
contact with real Indians; he had sung the praises of the natives
in his verses, but his knowledge derived almost entirely from
colonial chronicles.

The Brazilian Congress had appropriated three thousand pounds
sterling to outfit the "Argonauts of the Monkeys," as the illustrious members of the commission self-mockingly called themselves, and it was hoped that they would discover vast deposits
of coal, diamonds, or precious metals. Gonçalves Dias wrote
that just one lucky find could, almost overnight, "change the
face of Brazil" (Miguel-Pereira, 1943:242). The commission left
Rio with great fanfare at the end of January 1859, and arrived a
few weeks later in the coastal city of Fortaleza, the capital of
Ceará; this was to have been the jumping-off point for the expe-

dition, but chaotic disorganization and dissension detained it there for two and a half years. The expedition's funding was drastically reduced, and its members finally slipped aboard a ship for Rio in July 1861 – leaving behind great ill will, numerous unpaid bills, and assorted questions of paternity.

Gonçalves Dias, however, was determined to complete his immense assignment: to study every aspect of the Indians he encountered, to make measurements and molds of their bodies, to collect specimens of their clothing and utensils, to compute their total population, and to learn all of their languages (Miguel-Pereira, 1943:264). He traveled north to the Amazon, almost without money and accompanied only by a few servants, and stayed there for more than nine months. He was, however, profoundly depressed by the commission's failure and physically weakened by a long list of diseases, and he managed to collect only a limited number of artifacts. Even the land and its peoples appear to have made little impression on him, for his journals of this period are little more than careful computations of longitude and latitude (Miguel-Pereira, 1943:383–417). Part of this reticence was undoubtedly due to the poet's disillusionment with the Indians he met, so different from the proud natives of his verses. Although he gradually came to understand their way of life, he refused to admit that they were really Indians, and always referred to them as "blacks" or "half-breeds" (Miguel-Pereira, 1943:303).

Gonçalves Dias returned to Rio in November of 1861 – the artifacts he had gathered became the nucleus of the National Museum there – and immediately began to prepare a new escape. He sailed for Europe in April 1862, planning to take the waters at Vichy and Marienbad, but became convinced that he could die in peace only back in Maranhão. On 5 November 1864 the ship on which he was returning struck a reef within sight of the Maranhão coast, broke apart, and sank quickly; the crew escaped, but Gonçalves Dias was left to die.

The aristocrats of Maranhão still found it hard to accept Gonçalves Dias, despite his fame as the greatest poet the nation had produced, the most authentic voice of Brazil. Funds were raised to erect a memorial statue in São Luís, the provincial capital, and it was finally decided, after bitter debate, that the figure of the poet should look out over the sea. One wealthy contributor, whose mansion fronted on the square, was enraged by the decision. "And there's that damn little mulatto," he was heard to mutter, "standing with his back to me!" (Artur Azevedo, n.d.:173–7).

Gonçalves Dias left a considerable body of verse: some 220 lyrics and narratives, the first four cantos of an unfinished Indianist epic, *The Timbiras* (*Os Timbiras*), and numerous translations from European literature. The most interesting of his poems, both for his contemporaries and for modern students of Brazil, are those that deal with the Indian. Four Indianist poems appeared in his *First Songs* (*Primeiros Cantos*) of 1846, one in the *Second Songs* (*Segundos Cantos*) of 1848, and six more in the *Last Songs* (*Últimos Cantos*), published in 1851. The four extant cantos of *The Timbiras*, begun as early as 1847, were published in Leipzig in 1857.

Gonçalves Dias was very different from his European and American predecessors and contemporaries, whose Indianism was often simply an exotic backdrop or an excuse for philosophical speculation or nationalistic fervor. He was as certain as other members of the Brazilian Historical and Geographical Institute that the Indian could be a most useful national symbol, but his Indianism was also an intensely personal response to his own feelings of alienation and anxiety about his racial origins. He defined his role, as poet, as one of re-creation: "Homer created the world / A second time, Dante – Hell, / Milton – Paradise" (1959:156). Thus his Indianist epic, *The Timbiras*, was written as "an American Genesis – a Brazilian Iliad, a re-creation of Creation" (in Miguel-Pereira, 1943:88). Through these reconstructions of the lost world of Indian America – a world to which he belonged by virtue of his ancestry, but from which accidents of chronology and circumstance had exiled him – Gonçalves Dias sought to escape the white world of nineteenth-century Brazil.

In order to make the contours of his re-created Indian world as solid as possible, Gonçalves Dias poured over colonial accounts of native life, becoming Brazil's first serious enthnographer (Roquette-Pinto, 1948:86–7). Despite his close attention to accuracy and detail, however, his vision of the lost world was strongly colored by nineteenth-century ideals, by his feelings about the real Brazil around him, and by his own experiences.

Gonçalves Dias never sought to disguise the Indians' bellicosity, their sloth, their gluttony, or even their cannibalism, a practice carefully omitted by many of his contemporaries. He clearly believed, however, that the natives' virtues outweighed their faults. "The distinctive trait of the savage," he wrote, "is his love of independence and his disgust with any and all restraints. Liberty and space – that was his life" (1910:142). And, despite the violence of Indian life, there was also a strong cultural tradition that Gonçalves Dias felt was missing in nineteenth-century Brazil: "Among the Tupis," he declared, "everything was music and poetry; birth and death, war and feasts, love and religion, language and life – all was poetry" (1910:199).

A central figure in this poetic Indian world, the *piaga* or shaman, conformed closely to the Romantic ideal of the poet. The *piaga* was "at once the priest and the medicine-man, the seer and the bard of the natives of Brazil and of other parts of the Americas.... They were the object of everyone's devotion and respect; they were superior to the chiefs, the formidable boundary markers... between the known and the unknown" (1959:676–7). Perhaps the greatest tragedy of the Portuguese conquest, as Gonçalves Dias saw it, was that "even the Piaga shall become a slave" (1959:108).

The poet's vision of that conquest was black indeed: "It was greed disguised by a pretense of religion; it was an attack on the lords of the land, on the liberty of the Indians; there were convict colonists,... low and debased spirits who sought the forests in order to give free rein to the depravities of their brutal instincts" (1910:220). In seeking to explain the victory of these morally and physically inferior invaders from Europe, Gonçalves Dias focused on defects in the Indian world itself. He believed that fierce internal struggles between two native groups, the

Tupis and the Tapuias, blinded the natives to the danger from across the Atlantic. This interpretation had some basis in the colonial sources the poet consulted, but it was also strongly influenced by his view of contemporary Brazil. He was deeply worried by the civil disorders of the Regency, which he appears to have associated with the catastrophic disunity of the Indian world at the time of the conquest.

In describing the conflicts between Tupis and Tapuias, Gonçalves Dias consistently identified with the Tupis, and this is a most curious detail; it is clear that his mother and maternal grandmother were Gês, related to the Timbiras of Maranhão and classified as Tapuias by the earliest Europeans. Gonçalves Dias was certainly aware of these facts but – despite his usual insistence upon accuracy – refused to admit their validity. He described the Timbiras as Tupis, and the Timbira characters in his epic poem all have names adapted from the Tupi language. The reason for this ethnographic blind spot can be found, perhaps, in this passage from his comparative study of Brazil and Oceania: "The Tapuias differ from the Tupis because they belong to the Mongol race, while the latter offer analogies with certain of the branches of the Caucasian race" (1910:60). Even within the sheltered confines of his Indian dreamworld, Gonçalves Dias was still attempting to disguise his racial origins.

A second explanation of Portuguese success was the invaders' exploitation of Christianity, whose doctrines were naturally attractive to the noble natives of Brazil, as a means to the pacification and eventual destruction of the Indian. In the subtle and symbolic "Indian's Song" ("O Canto do Indio"), a brave laments his transformation from a virile and self-confident warrior into a servile, love-sick swain – all because he has caught a single glimpse of a white girl bathing in a forest stream (1959:108–10). Enamored of her ivory neck and golden ringlets, he declares himself ready to sacrifice his tribe, his religion, and freedom itself in order to win her love. The poet's use of capitalization in this poem, however, makes it clear that the Indian's physical passion for the woman he calls "the Virgin of the Christians" is a metaphor for the destructive appeal of Christianity itself.

Miscegenation, then, appears in "The Indian's Song" as synonymous with social and cultural change – an equation that was to become a fundamental idea in Brazilian letters. The same theme also appears, in a less ideological and far more personal form, in "Marabá," one of Gonçalves Dias' most famous poems. The half-breed girl called Marabá, a classic European beauty, is an alien outcast in the Indian world – a neatly ironic reversal of Gonçalves Dias' own situation in the salons of Rio de Janeiro:

> I live and am lonely, unwanted and hated!
> Was I not created
> By our God, Tupã?
> If one of the warriors does deign to approach me,
> It is to reproach me:
> "You are Marabá!"
>
> My hair falls in waves of soft yellow ringlets;
> The purest of gold dust does not gleam so bright.
> The winds of the forest, entranced by its beauty,
> Find it as golden as a hummingbird's flight.
>
> But the warriors reply: "Your long, golden hair
> Perhaps may be fair,
> But is tangled in curls, for you are Marabá;
> We love hair as straight as an arrow in flight,
> Black as the night,
> Long and smooth-flowing, not gold as the day."
>
> And the soft words of love I have held deep inside me
> Silent shall lie;
> And the garland I weave for a warrior who loves me
> Shall wither and die.
>
> And never a warrior shall gently uncover
> My body's frail bloom;
> I live in my loneliness, sobbing self-pity –
> The Marabá's doom![1]

Just beneath the irony, however, is the poet's anguished realization that his exile is total – that, despite his search for solace in a carefully and lovingly re-created Indian world, he would be a *marabá*, an outcast, there as well. His bitterness cries out in the dry explanation of the poem's title presented in his notes:

We find, in the *Chronicle of the Company* [an early history of the Jesuit missions in Brazil], a passage which explains the meaning of this word, and the idea of this brief composition. "A certain old [Indian] woman had taken a child, the son of her daughter-in-law, and buried it alive as soon as it was born, for it was the child of what they call *marabá*, which means of mixed blood – something detested by these people." [1959:679]

Gonçalves Dias' attitudes toward his Portuguese and African ancestors, Bilac's other sad races, are just as complex as those found in his Indianist works. One of his friends wrote that the poet's African blood was "the torment of his life; it was the thought that covered his heart with clouds during nights of insomnia; it was the recollection that came, from time to time, to awaken him from his dreams of glory" (in Miguel-Pereira, 1943:14). But although Gonçalves Dias declared his opposition to the idea of slavery (1909:4–89), he was himself a slave owner, and he never identified himself, even obliquely, with Brazil's black population. Moreover, his comments on the Melanesians were intensely racist: "Experience shows that the black race, in contact with any other, always allows itself to be subjugated, which is proof of incontestable inferiority" (1910:353).

Gonçalves Dias' feelings about the Portuguese were even more ambivalent: He detested them for their destruction of the Indian world and for their long domination of Brazil, emotions bound up with his resentment of his own father, but his many friends and colleagues in Portugal and the heroic saints and warriors of Portugal's precolonial, medieval past remained outside the range of his nationalistic animus. The *Sestets of Brother Antony* (*Sextilhas de Frei Antão*), begun early in 1847 and published in the *Second Songs*, are the poet's most curious literary production (1959:283–348). Critics have generally interpreted the *Sestets* as a prideful attempt to prove that a Brazilian – a half-breed Brazilian, at that – could write perfect medieval Portuguese. A closer look at the poems, however, suggests that they were far more than the simple "philological practice" Gonçalves Dias claimed (Miguel-Pereira, 1943:116).

The *Sestets* are an elegiac re-creation of another lost world, the crusading Portugal of the reigns of Afonso V and João II (1438–95)

– just before the discovery and destruction of Indian Brazil.
Gonçalves Dias makes gentle fun of some aspects of this era, but
its values and its heroes are remarkably similar to his image of
Indian Brazil. This medieval world was even more distant from
the reality of nineteenth-century Brazil than the forests of the
Tupis, moreover, and Gonçalves Dias – completely hidden from
view by the persona of Brother Antony, his own voice drowned
out by a mass of archaic verbiage – felt free to discuss one of his
major preoccupations, miscegenation, and to come face to face
at last with his African ancestors.

The Africans in the *Sestets* are presented as magnificently handsome and heroic Moors, more than equal to any Portuguese.
Brother Antony admits that even he was moved to lust by the
charms of one North African captive, Gulnare, totally forgetting
his vows of chastity; Gulnare's brave African lover, Mustafá,
contrasts the friar's weakness with the purity of the holy men of
Islam. Mustafá is very proud of both his color and his race:
"Whatever God does is well done," he proclaims; "I was born a
Moor, not made!" (1959:317). The two Africans are eventually
converted to Christianity and freed to live happily amidst general admiration and respect; when Mustafá dies, Gulnare becomes a saintly nun. Gonçalves Dias made a similar point in
another sestet, describing the love and happy marriage of the
bravest of all Portuguese knights, Gonçalo Hermigues, and another beautiful North African captive (1959:333–48). In the poet's
version of medieval Portugal, in short, Africans are not degraded
slaves, but worthy enemies and beloved companions; love between members of different races is sanctified by the church and
glorified as the work of God.

The most famous and enduring of Gonçalves Dias' elegies for
lost worlds, the "Song of Exile" ("Canção do Exílio"), was written in Portugal during July of 1843, when he was only nineteen.
The poem was reprinted, shortly after its publication in the poet's
First Songs of 1846, in tiny provincial magazines and newspapers, and became part of the stock-in-trade of every local orator.
Several musical versions of the poem have achieved great popularity, and part of the "Song of Exile" passed directly into the

folk tradition as a children's game-song (Bandeira, 1958:II, 667).
Even today, it is the single most popular Brazilian poem, and
most Brazilians – rich or poor, literate or illiterate – know it by
heart; its recitation can still move listeners to tears.

It is worthwhile to look closely at the "Song of Exile," in the
original and in translation, in order to define what it meant to
Gonçalves Dias and what it has come to mean to Brazilians in
the decades since its publication (1959:103):

> Minha terra tem palmeiras
> Onde canta o Sabiá;
> As aves, que aqui gorjeiam,
> Não gorjeiam como lá.
>
> Nosso céu tem mais estrêlas,
> Nossas várzeas tem mais flôres,
> Nossos bosques tem mais vida,
> Nossa vida mais amôres.
>
> Em cismar, sòzinho, à noite,
> Mais prazer encontro eu lá;
> Minha terra tem palmeiras,
> Onde canta o Sabiá.
>
> Minha terra tem primores,
> Que tais não encontro eu cá;
> Em cismar – sòzinho, à noite –
> Mais prazer encontro eu lá;
> Minha terra tem palmeiras,
> Onde canta o Sabiá.
>
> Não permita Deus que eu morra,
> Sem que eu volte para lá;
> Sem que desfrute os primores
> Que não encontro por cá;
> Sem qu'inda aviste as palmeiras,
> Onde canta o Sabiá.
>
> There are palm trees in my country,
> And the singing Sabiá;
> The birds warbling here
> Don't sing as they do there.
>
> Our heavens have more stars,
> Our meadows far more blooms,
> Our forests have more life,
> Our life has much more love.

When I dream, alone, at night,
I find more pleasure there;
There are palm trees in my country
And the singing Sabiá.

My country has a loveliness
That I don't find here;
When I dream – alone, at night –
I find more pleasure there;
There are palm trees in my country,
And the singing Sabiá.

May God not let me perish
Without going back there;
Without knowing the loveliness
I cannot find here;
Without a glimpse of palm trees
And the singing Sabiá.

The "Song of Exile" would seem, at first glance, to be a simple expression of the young poet's longing for Brazil. On closer examination, however, it becomes clear that the land Gonçalves Dias longed to regain – as he described it – was *not* the Brazil of the middle of the nineteenth century. There are no cities, no trace of civilization; this is the virgin world before the coming of the Europeans, and the world of his own lost childhood. The "Song of Exile" describes a specific geographical area: The meadows (*várzeas*) and the *bosques* – small, orderly groves of trees – are not the Amazonian jungle, but the interior of Maranhão, the area around the Quinta da Boa Vista ("Farm of the Lovely View") where Gonçalves Dias was born and spent the first and happiest years of his life with his *cafuza* mother and his Gê grandmother.[2] The poet's recollection of this land of his childhood and of his Indian heritage, however, was inevitably flawed; he had lived in the town of Caxias from the age of six on, and his father and stepmother had probably restricted his contact with the wilderness so closely identified with Vicência. The kind of *sabiá* – a variety of thrush, popularized by Gonçalves de Magalhães as Brazil's answer to the European nightingale – that makes its nests in palm trees is, in fact, the only *sabiá* that does not sing at all (Ricardo, 1955:675).

One reason for the emotional force of the "Song of Exile" is the leanness of its vocabulary. Gonçalves Dias never qualifies or describes, and his presentation of his dreamworld merely lists its characteristics – its stars, its woods, its meadows. The traditional *ufanista* themes of Brazil's vastness and abundance are repeated here, but in the simplest, most direct form: more stars, more flowers, more life, more love. The land's inhabitants, who might not be equal to the beauty and richness around them, are safely hidden from our view.

Of equal importance, and far more subtle, are the metrics of the poem. The structure of Portuguese verse is based upon the number of syllables in a line, but the natural accents of the words can be used to form patterns of stress – the metrical feet that appear in English verse. Gonçalves Dias used these rhythmic cells of two to three syllables to give a strong subliminal texture; his favorite rhythm in most of his Indianist poems, the anapest, was intended to suggest strength, virility, and the beating of distant drums.

Each of the lines in the "Song of Exile" has seven syllables, but there is also a strong natural stress rhythm – trochaic tetrameter. This rhythmic pattern continues throughout the poem, but breaks down in three places. In the third line of the first stanza, where Portugal (*aqui*, "here") is mentioned for the first time, the poem departs sharply from the model; the regular sequence is restored in the fourth line, which mentions Brazil (*lá*, "there"). This is not simply coincidental; the same breakdown in the stress rhythm happens the next time Portugal (*cá*, "here") appears, in the first two lines of the fourth stanza. In the last lines of the poem, the rhythm breaks again, more drastically, as the poet fears that he will never return from exile; the final line of the refrain, when the *sabiá* sings, restores the rhythm. Through these metrical shifts, consciously or unconsciously, Gonçalves Dias managed to suggest his misery in Portugal and his longing for the lost world of Brazil, making the reader alternately uneasy or content.

The poet's attitude, in the "Song of Exile," is almost entirely passive. Several lines – notably stanza three, line two, and stanza

four, lines two and four – contain the first-person singular subject pronoun, *eu*, where it is not necessary either for meaning or
for metrics. Normally, of course, *eu* is an important part of speech,
receiving heavy stress; as Gonçalves Dias placed it in the poem,
however, it not only lacks accentual force, but is even absorbed
by elision into the last syllable of the preceding word. This un-
usual placement of the pronoun influences the reader, identify-
ing with the poet, to feel overwhelmed and lost.[3]

The "Song of Exile," then, expressed several overlapping levels
of alienation for Gonçalves Dias: the simple nostalgia of a young
man far from his native country; the acute sense of exile from his
origins and from his early childhood; the bitter alienation of a
self-conscious half-breed. The poem, the product of the poet's
own suffering, nevertheless appealed, through its simplicity and
its deliberate vagueness, to the general disquiet of his contemporaries in Brazil. Independence had not assuaged the sense of
exile evident in the writings of the colonial period, nor had it
changed the profound concern that Brazil, as a nation, might
not be equal to the glories of its landscape. Gonçalves Dias'
readers, therefore, were eager to take emotional refuge in the
nebulous and ethereal dreamworld of the "Song of Exile," and
in the more detailed worlds of Indian Brazil and medieval Portugal that he re-created in other poems.

The "Indian fever" of Gonçalves Dias' era was relatively short-
lived, but the "Song of Exile" still retains its emotional power for
Brazilians, cutting across racial and social divisions and meaning
different things to different readers. For whites, the dreamworld
is the prospect of a whitened, European, modernized Brazil;
nonwhite readers and admirers of the poem can share the alienation Gonçalves Dias felt as a *marabá* in a world dominated by
whiteness, and can dream of a more equal society. Above all,
the poem's simple phrases still appeal to all those who feel
themselves exiled from the ideal Brazil, the great nation worthy
of the immensity and perfection of its land.

3

The novelist as matchmaker: José de Alencar

José de Alencar (1829–77) is the other great figure of Brazilian Indianism. His utilization of Brazil's Indian past was less personal than that of Gonçalves Dias, and more consciously ideological. Indianism was simply a logical and effective strategy in the struggle to create a meaningful and complete national history, to establish a consciousness of national separateness and worth, and to defend that new identity against powerful cultural pressures from abroad. Alencar defined Brazilian culture as an infant; it had not yet, he declared in 1872, found "writers who can give it the finishing touches and create a true national aesthetic, silencing those – today so vigorous – who would seek to recolonize our hearts and souls, something force of arms can no longer accomplish" (1967:VI, 166).

For Alencar, the Indian world was "the cradle of our nationhood" (1967:I, 376), rather than the tomb of a race. The representation and idealization of that world was an essential step in the creation of a literature "inherently Brazilian in inspiration and in form" (in Gomes, 1958:14). Alencar's three nativist novels – *The Guarani Indian* (*O Guarani*), *Iracema*, and *Ubirajara* – were founded upon a purposefully unrealistic and ahistorical vision of a Brazilian Middle Ages; "the rules of chivalry," he insisted, "in the days when European knighthood was in flower, most assuredly did not surpass the gallantry of the savages of Brazil in either dignity or mettle" (in Proença, 1972:42).

Alencar also remains far more popular than Gonçalves Dias and the other Indianists; the "Song of Exile" has survived, but other works the movement produced are rarely read. Alencar's novels, and his Indianist works in particular, have had a remarkably enduring appeal. Proof of this timeless popularity are the dozens of editions of his novels – more than a hundred editions of *Iracema* alone are said to have been published (Alencar, 1967:I, 250) – and the statistics of lending libraries (Heron de Alencar, 1956:863) and the tens of thousands of Brazilians baptized with names taken from Alencar's novels.[1]

Alencar felt free to praise the Indian and to deal openly and positively with Indian–Portuguese miscegenation. Gonçalves Dias' reticence and evasiveness reflected his preoccupation with his own humble and tainted origins. Alencar, on the other hand, was the son of one of the founding fathers of independent Brazil and a member of one of the most powerful traditional families of the Northeast; in short, he belonged to the inner circle of the elite. Nor was he a typical Romantic, a purposefully marginal and tragic figure. Alencar seems to have been a "normal man, leading a full and apparently unclouded life; the fact that he died of tuberculosis is due more to the backwardness of medicine in his time than to Romanticism" (Proença, 1972:7). He had a privileged childhood, a stable and seemingly contented marriage, and almost total freedom from financial pressures. Moreover, Alencar was almost immediately successful in every career he tried: journalism, law, letters, administration, and public service.

This is not to say that Alencar was a warm and sympathetic person; despite the best efforts of his biographers, he often comes across as a humorless, nasty little man. In the words of a contemporary, "the impression one gets, when one first meets him – this small and apparently testy man, his face hidden behind a thick beard – is of fear rather than pleasure or respect. Testy, proud, harsh, almost misanthropic" (in Menezes, 1965:72). Alencar was also terribly diligent, very sure of himself and of his ideas, and often petty in his relationships with literary and political colleagues. He went out of his way to antagonize many of his contemporaries, including the emperor, Pedro II, and constantly complained of dark conspiracies against him both as a writer and as a public figure.

Gonçalves de Magalhães, the founder of ˋBrazilian Romanticism, published his long-awaited epic poem, *The Confederation of the Tamoio Indians* (*A Confederação dos Tamoios*) in 1856. Alencar, under the pseudonym "Ig.," attacked the epic in a series of letters published in the *Diário do Rio de Janeiro*, denouncing both its conception and its style. The powerful old guard of Romanticism vehemently defended Magalhães; even Pedro II, under a discreet pseudonym, came to the aid of his old friend and adviser. Alencar's attacks continued, however, mixing common sense, nationalistic bravado, and slashing sarcasm. As the true identity of "Ig." became known, the controversy established Alencar – at the age of twenty-six – as a major literary figure; it also earned him a number of fervent enemies (Castello, 1953).

Alencar's first complete novel, *Five Minutes* (*Cinco Minutos*), was serialized in the *Diário* in the last days of 1856. Early in 1857, he began serialization of two new novels, *The Little Widow* (*A Viuvinha*) and *The Guarani Indian*. The first of these disappeared from the *Diário* after a few chapters, but the other was an astonishing success. A contemporary later recalled that

> the whole of Rio de Janeiro, so to speak, was reading *The Guarani Indian*, following with rapt suspense the pure and discreet affection of Ceci and Peri...In São Paulo,...large numbers of students gathered at every boarding-house that could boast of a lucky subscriber to the *Diário*; they all listened, open-mouthed and deeply shaken from time to time by a sort of electric shock, as the student with the strongest voice read aloud. [In Proença, 1971:47–8]

During the next eight years, Alencar published the rest of *The Little Widow* and two other novels of contemporary urban life (*Lucíola* and *Diva*), another "aboriginal," Indianist novel (*Iracema*), and one historical novel of the colonial past, *The Silver Mines* (*As Minas de Prata*). He also wrote five plays and an assortment of essays, and began a new career as a bureaucrat in the Ministry of Justice. He had been thinking about going into politics as well, and returned to Ceará in 1860, after his father's death, and ran for the Chamber of Deputies. He went on to a distinguished if polemical career as deputy, senator, and minister of justice – all the while continuing to write novels.

As he looked back on his literary career, during the last years of his life, Alencar wanted to believe that he had set out from the very beginning to create the Brazilian novel, working in four subgenres: the aboriginal novel, the historical novel, the novel of urban life, and the novel of rural life (Alencar, 1967:VI, 165–7). This sequence was designed to unify the nation chronologically – spanning its entire history from Indians to Empire – and physically; the novels were to include descriptions of landscapes and customs from every major geographical region. It is far more likely, however, that Alencar's concept of the national literature and of the novel developed rather slowly during the period from 1856 to 1865.

The question of the form the new literature of independent Brazil should take preoccupied Alencar throughout his life. His first consideration of this topic can be seen in his 1856 articles criticizing *The Confederation of the Tamoio Indians*. His chief complaint was that the epic form, at least in this particular case, was both obsolete and unworthy of the subject matter. The glories of a new and virginal land, he declared, required "some celestial song, some original harmony never yet dreamed of by the aged literature of an aged world" (1960:IV, 865). What was needed was something new, "a truly national poem, in which everything would be new, from idea to form, from image to meter. The poetic form Homer used to sing of the Greeks," Alencar went on, "cannot sing of the Indians; the meter that told of the sufferings of Troy and of mythological struggles cannot express the sorrowful threnodies of Guanabara and the savage creeds of America. Can it be that the formless chaos of the human mind does not contain a new form of poetry, a new meter for verse?" (1960:875–6).

Alencar was still dreaming of a "truly national poem" in 1863, seven years later, when he began to work seriously on his own Indianist epic, *The Children of the God Tupã* (*Os Filhos de Tupã*). He found the task extremely frustrating and a great deal more difficult than he had supposed, and he did not finish the epic. The fragments he completed are no better than the *Confederation*, and clearly inferior to Gonçalves Dias' unfinished *The Timbira Indians*. Alencar's conviction that his enormous success as a novelist would not be complete without an epic to his credit is evidence both of the power of the tradition of Camões and of a generalized uncertainty about the place of prose fiction in Brazilian literature. Alencar concluded, in 1873, that the novel was indeed the new form he had demanded in 1856, the true "poem of real life," but the title of the essay which contains that declaration – "How and Why I Am a Novelist" ("Como e Porque sou Romancista") – reflects his insecurity, his need to explain that choice of genre (1967:I, lxxiii).

Back in 1856, Alencar was only subliminally conscious of the existence of a possible prose alternative to the Indianist epic. He praised the exotic novels of Chateaubriand and declared that "if

Walter Scott were to recast these verses [those of Magalhães] in his own elegant and correct style; if he were to turn this poem into a novel, he would give it such charm and appeal that any reader who flipped through the first pages would be compelled to read the entire book with pleasure and interest" (1960:IV, 893).

It is not surprising that Alencar thought of the novel only in terms of its French and British exponents. At that time, dozens of pirated translations of European novels were serialized in Brazilian newspapers, and local publishing houses turned out their own unauthorized versions of foreign best sellers.[2] The number of serialized translations began to drop off slowly during the forties, as the first Brazilian efforts in the genre appeared, but the popularity and ready availability of works by more prestigious European competitors continued to haunt Brazil's novelists for decades.

The popular success of even the most inferior foreign novels is not, however, the only explanation for the agonizingly slow development of prose fiction in Brazil. Many Brazilians were biased against the genre for social and intellectual reasons; there also appears to have been a considerable confusion about the relationship between fantasy and reality in novels set in Brazil. First, as Antônio Cândido noted, educated Brazilians saw the novel as "a lesser genre, one for which Rhetoric and Poetics – the basis for their knowledge of literature – had not prepared them. A kind of brilliant bastard offspring, lacking tradition and rules, and dangerously appealing to popular taste" (1975:II, 119).

Secondly, the natural market for the Brazilian novel was socially and geographically limited. The most popular novelist of the forties and early fifties, Joaquim Manuel de Macedo (1820–82), wrote for and about the members of the new urbanized upper middle class that began to develop in Rio de Janeiro around 1840: doctors, lawyers, public functionaries, and, in particular, the wives and daughters of these prosperous burghers. The novel was still almost unknown outside the larger cities of the coast; in the interior, it was regarded as dangerously immoral by conservative fathers and husbands. Elizabeth Agassiz recalled that

on one occasion, when staying at a fazenda, I took up a volume
which was lying on the piano...As I stood turning over the leaves (it
proved to be a romance), the master of the house came up, and
remarked that the book was not suitable reading for ladies, but that
here (putting into my hand a small volume) was a work adapted
to the use of women and children, which he had provided for the se-
nhoras of his family. I opened it, and found it to be a sort of textbook of morals, filled with commonplace sentiments, copybook phrases,
written in a tone of condescending indulgence for the feminine
intellect. [Agassiz and Agassiz, 1886:480]

Defenders of the novel insisted upon its pedagogical and ethical potential: "It is," J. C. Fernandes Pinheiro wrote in 1855,
"agreeable reading, and, we might almost say, easily digestible
pap for those with weak stomachs. Through it, the moral and
intellectual level of the populace may be raised, allowing our
people to learn some metaphysical truths which would otherwise escape their understanding. If the theater has justly been
called a school for behavior, the novel is morality in action" (in
Cândido, 1975:II, 119).

This emphasis upon the instructional possibilities of the novel
coincided with uncertainty about the fictive nature of the genre
in the Brazilian context. A romance, by definition, should contain fantastic and exotic elements, raising the reader above the
banalities of everyday life. At the same time, the reader should
be able to identify with the characters as real people, and the
action should always remain within the realm of the possible
and the moral in order to maintain involvement and avoid corrupting
the innocent. Imported novels enjoyed a clearly unfair advan-
tage, given these strictures, since works set in other times and
other landscapes, whether the banks of the Mississippi or the
alleys of Paris, automatically reached an acceptable level of fantasy for Brazilian readers. At the same time the inherent exoticism of these alien settings greatly expanded the limits of
verisimilitude and decency, so that physically impossible or morally reprehensible events could be described.

Precisely because they were writing about contemporary Brazil, the authors of the first sentimental novels of the forties and

fifties were judged by a double standard: They were dealing with settings and mores their readers knew well, and they therefore had to be exact in their descriptions and realistic and circumspect in their plotting. When Alencar wrote a novel and two plays about prostitution, he discovered that the heroine of *La dame aux camèlies*, for example, was a cautionary model for the young, her sinfulness attenuated and excused by the alien milieu in which she moved; the most moralistic description of a real Brazilian prostitute, however golden her heart, was a scandalous, even criminal affront to public morality and decency (Menezes, 1965:157–62).

The only way Brazilian novelists could cope with this double standard, ironically, was to emphasize the verisimilitude of the events they described while constantly stressing the fictive nature of the narrative voice – a voice clearly not their own. The solution, then, was the frame – or, in Alencar's urban novels, a set of frames. Macedo's most popular tale, *The Little Brunette (A Moreninha)*, was structured as a true story, written to satisfy a wager by the fictional narrator who is also one of the major characters in that story. Alencar's first urban romance, *Five Minutes*, was published anonymously; it is dedicated to D***, a female cousin of the fictional narrator, who is also the hero. Alencar's second effort, *The Little Widow*, is similarly dedicated to D*** and has the same narrator, who reveals that he knows the story of Jorge and Carolina only because he and his wife Carlota – whom he met and married in *Five Minutes* – are their neighbors and good friends. Alencar's two other early novels in the "Female Profiles" series, *Lucíola* and *Diva*, also share a single complex frame.

When Alencar began writing *Five Minutes*, late in 1856, he had already experimented successfully with the creation of a fictional voice in a nonfictional setting. "Ig.,' the pseudonymous author of the *Letters on the Confederation*, was an invented character with his own style and his own implicit biography. "I wanted," Alencar later revealed, "to remain totally unknown, and – in order to draw all suspicion away from myself, the editor of the paper – I pretended to be an old man who played ombre in the evenings and who had once, long ago, visited Europe" (in Menezes, 1965: 104). The unnamed author of Alencar's weekly column of *crônicas*, "As the Pen Writes" ("Ao Correr da Pena"), was another created persona – witty, lighthearted, and irreverent, fond of bad puns and gallicisms, skipping blithely from gossip to fashion to the Crimean War: in short, a character very different from the serious, withdrawn, and nationalistic Alencar.

In writing *Five Minutes* and *The Little Widow*, Alencar delineated his vision of the novel and its social function. Because his first romances were written for serialization, his chapters tend to be roughly uniform in length; the reader's interest is maintained through regular cycles of joy and despair, of mystery and revelation, which generally conform to the chapter divisions. Alencar was the first Brazilian novelist to structure the flow of fictional events with such intelligence and precision. He also insisted, through his narrators and frames, that all the events recounted were fact rather than fiction. "I'm not writing a romance," the narrator of *The Little Widow* tells D***; "I'm telling you a story. Truth makes verisimilitude unnecessary" (1967:VI, 64).

As he turned out these stories of urban life, Alencar found that even the relatively narrow confines of the short novel still allowed him to pursue two interrelated goals, describing and instructing. He saw it as his responsibility to create a "true national taste" through the careful and exact description of all things truly Brazilian, from the primeval forest to the rosewood furniture in the parlor. His compatriots should be taught to appreciate the perfection of their land. At the same time, he was determined to convince his readers of the importance of the traditional virtues of Brazilian society, as he defined them: patriotic fervor, hard work, courage in the face of adversity, marital trust and fidelity, love of family, thrift, and simplicity. These values, he felt, were menaced by the attractions of "foreign ways and customs" and threatened by the amoral rapacity of European capitalism.

In his novels and in his plays, also didactic in nature and purpose, Alencar departed in one important respect from this traditional patriarchal ethic: His heroes and heroines fall deeply and passionately in love on their own, and this idealized, romantic love is set in opposition to the arranged marriages of the past. This espousal of romantic love was not entirely original; Macedo had dared, a decade earlier, to allow his middle-class characters to meet and fall in love without parental intervention. Alencar, however, went a great deal further to explore the ultimate consequences of this shift in courtship and marriage patterns.

The primary consequence was the necessary liberalization of traditional constraints on the freedom of movement of females. Foreign visitors to imperial Brazil regularly noted the "limited, imprisoned existence" of Brazilian women, surrounded by "repression and constraint" and unable to venture outside their homes, "except under certain conditions, without awakening scandal" (Agassiz and Agassiz, 1886:479). If young men and women were not allowed to meet each other more freely and naturally than the traditional honor code permitted, they could not hope to find the one great love that destiny ordained.

Relationships between the sexes, in Alencar's view, should be based upon virtue, decency, and mutual respect; this new, higher morality required that women be both better educated and more sophisticated, able to read and to learn from the examples of proper and improper conduct that literature could provide. And, finally, the traditional victims of dishonor and degradation, prostitutes and courtesans, had to be allowed to redeem themselves through virtue, true love, and the saving grace of maternity.

Alencar presented this mix of traditional virtues and the new morality of romantic love within a standardized plot structure. He first introduced his hero and heroine, grabbing the reader's attention by placing these two characters in an inherently scandalous situation – the hanky-panky in the back of the bus in *Five Minutes*, for example – that defied, however innocently, the old morality. Once he had matched his lovers and established the force of their passion, Alencar revealed an apparently insuperable obstacle that stood in the way of their happiness. This obstacle, the love problem the characters must resolve, is physical in

Five Minutes, but it is more often social or moral, based upon a serious disparity in the status or character of the lovers.

The source of this disparity is almost always economic: The heroine is beautiful and rich; the hero is handsome and intelligent, but poor by birth or by unhappy accident. In Alencar's terms, poverty is the greatest curse that a man can suffer (1967:VI, 46). This financial imbalance must be resolved before the lovers can marry, and Alencar clearly enjoyed the conflict more than the happy ending, savoring the twists and turns of the plot and maintaining the love problem until the last two or three pages; the denouement is often, in fact, a kind of last-minute postscript.

The resolution of the imbalance depends almost entirely upon the actions and character of the heroine, always the most forceful and interesting figure in the book. She raises the hero out of poverty, or motivates him to raise himself; she teaches him to assert himself, to value love, decency, and simplicity, and to appreciate the unspoiled nature of Brazil. In return for his redemption, the hero must suffer privations, humiliations, or the pangs of jealousy.

Even in *Lucíola*, where Lúcia the courtesan appears to be the social and moral inferior of the hero, she is nonetheless pure at heart, and her chaste alter ego – Maria da Graça, still present within her personality despite her suffering and perversion – allows Lúcia to redeem herself before she dies. At the same time, however, Lúcia/Maria is also, by her example, restoring the hero's lost innocence and teaching him to value decency and simplicity, so that he will be a suitable husband for the chaste younger sister she has raised and educated. As Lúcia/Maria gives her sister to a reborn Paulo, she also frees him from financial worries by leaving him the large fortune she has earned through vice.

As this analysis suggests, the heroine is the central figure in Alencar's urban novels. He saw women as the focus of Brazilian life, and although he strongly supported improved education for all the inhabitants of the nation, he stressed that the education of females was an overriding goal – and not merely because he wished thereby to increase the market for his own novels, so that "instead of some ten million inhabitants with only one reader for every thousand illiterates, we will have the kind of audience for our books that writers in the United States have for theirs" (in Gomes, 1958:12).

The education of women was vital, in Alencar's vision of society, because they unified Brazil in three essential areas. First, they were the leveling agents of social change: A good marriage could raise a man's economic and social status; an unscrupulous courtesan could destroy him morally and financially. Secondly, if women unified Brazilian society by harmonizing economic disparity, they also – as "apostles of civilization" (Alencar, 1960:IV, 168) – could unify the nation morally and culturally. With the education of women, "civilization would reach even the lowest classes; the family itself would be a school for learning and morality" (1960:IV, 169). And, finally, women as mothers unified the nation chronologically, linking one generation to the next and transmitting the values of the past to Brazilians of the future.

Alencar's novels of contemporary urban life brought him great success, particularly among female readers in the cities; his Indianist novels revolutionized the genre and established his preeminence as the nation's most popular novelist. His great discovery, probably an unconscious one at first, took place sometime in the last months of 1856: He began to realize that it was possible to combine the descriptive and instructive functions of the urban novel with the idea he had set forth, a few months earlier, in his critique of the *Confederation*: the patriotic responsibility of Brazil's new national literature to glorify the colonial and precolonial past.

The first product of this realization, *The Guarani Indian* (1857), singlehandedly created the Brazilian Indianist novel, fusing a flamboyantly unrealistic vision of the past with the standard plot structure and the concrete moral and social concerns of his sentimental tales. This leap into the past, to the early seventeenth century, separated Alencar from the events he described and allowed him to discard the frame of the pseudonymous internal narrator. It also freed him from the strictures of verisimilitude and enabled him to raise his basic plot – the hero and heroine struggling to overcome the love problem – to the level of myth.

José de Alencar was accused, late in his career, of plagiarizing his Indianist novels from the works of Chateaubriand and Cooper. He admitted the influence of *Atala*, but argued quite correctly that the form and spirit of his own works owed little to that model. The charge that *The Guarani Indian* imitated *The Last of the Mohicans*, however, greatly disturbed him. As Alencar explained, "Brazil, like the United States, has...a period of conquest, in which the invading race destroys the indigenous race. This struggle creates analogous situations, owing to the similarity of the natives...But this convergence derives from history; it is predestined, and is not the result of imitation" (1967:I, lxxxii).

Despite this declaration, the basic situation in *The Guarani Indian* does appear superficially similar to that of Cooper's novel. Dom António de Mariz and his family are beseiged by hostile Indians and by the treachery of some of their own allies. The household includes Dom António's blonde and beautiful daughter Cecília (Cooper's Alice Munro) and his "niece," the dark and sultry Isabel (Cora Munro), who is really his illegitimate daughter by an Indian woman. Any reader familiar with *The Last of the Mohicans* automatically assumes the rest of the plot: Cecília will be won by a gallant white warrior; Isabel will arouse the passions of a Good Indian and a Bad Indian, but all three must die at the end in order to preserve the purity of white America.

Alencar, however, destroys all our preconceived notions. Dark Isabel's chosen mate is Álvaro, the noble Portuguese youth, but he is killed by the Indians and Isabel takes poison to join him in death. Fair Cecília's true love, it turns out, is Peri, portrayed as the most handsome, noble, and courageous of Indians. She and Peri are the focus of the novel, the lovers who must overcome the love problem, here their racial and cultural differences; this disparity is the historical equivalent of the poverty of Alencar's

urban heroes. Peri's adoration of Cecília changes him and nar-
rows the disparity; her love and instruction civilize and convert
him, moving him along the racial continuum to whiteness. It is
Peri alone who can descend unharmed into the symbolic pit of
reptiles that guards Cecília's purity, and he alone can retrieve
her lost jewel.

This is only one of the fantastic feats that love for Cecília
enables Peri to perform. He is far stronger than any of Alencar's
contemporary heroes, but he too must suffer and sacrifice before
Cecília's love can raise and redeem him. His name for the girl is
"Ceci," a standard nickname for Cecília; Alencar explains, however, that in the Indian tongue *ceci* is an infinitive: "to feel pain,
to suffer" (1967:I, 87–8).

Alencar wrote *The Guarani Indian* for serialization, turning out
about a chapter a day under great pressure. He insisted that he
had no clear idea of how the book would turn out; he felt that
the characters almost wrote their own story (1967:I, lxxviii–lxxxix).
That story was very long indeed, by the standards of the contemporary Brazilian novel, and the plot was far more complex
than that of any previous national work in the genre. What held
his readers' attention in 1857, however – the efforts of Peri and
Ceci to overcome their love problem – still interests and moves
Brazilians.

The final resolution of their disparity is the first created etiological myth in Brazilian literature, a fusion of Christian and
Indian traditions. Peri saves Cecília when the hostile natives
launch their last and most deadly attack on Dom António's fort.
The Indians set fire to that structure, dancing "like diabolical
spirits in the flames of Hell" (1967:I, 223), and Dom António sets
off the powder supply, blowing up defender and attacker alike.
Peri and Ceci are the only survivors; all the other inhabitants of
the forest, red and white, have perished in the explosion and
conflagration.

A sudden flash flood forces the pair to abandon their canoe
and take refuge at the top of a large palm tree. As the water
rises, Peri tells the white girl the story of Tamandaré, an Indian

culture hero who long ago took refuge with his beloved in another palm tree. God had decreed the destruction of a heedless world, and all other humans died in the Deluge; only Tamandaré and his mate survived to repeople the earth.

Peri somehow manages to uproot the palm tree that shelters him and Ceci, and they sail down the river on it, swept along by the current and by the sudden realization of their love for each other. Cecília tries to convince herself that she loves Peri only as a brother, and dreams of union with him only after death, in heaven. Peri, however, insists that they will survive the flood, and Alencar carefully allows the reader to choose between Ceci's timorous and conventional ending and Peri's alternative – the survival and fusion, in some Edenic refuge, of the best of Europe and of Indian America, leading implicity to the creation of a new, Brazilian race.

Alencar returned twice to the Indianist novel after failing to complete his verse epic of native life. The last of these works, *Ubirajara* (1874), is the least interesting of the three. It deals with a familiar situation, only slightly altered: The heroic brave, Ubirajara, loves and is loved by two Indian maidens, Jandira, from his own tribe, and Araci, the princess of his sworn enemies. Alencar had become extremely sensitive to charges that the native world he had created was ethnologically false, and this novel – set before the arrival of Europeans – sometimes offers more erudition than enjoyment. The novel's appeal was weakened, in particular, by its ending. The resolution Alencar found for the parallel love problems of the three principal characters was so authentic that it fell entirely outside the experience and the ethics of his readers: Ubirajara defeats his enemies, is proclaimed chief of both tribes, and pacifies and unifies the Indian world by marrying *both* girls.

Iracema (1865), Alencar's other Indianist novel, is his masterpiece, a subtle and innovative fusion of reality and myth. He called the book a "legend," but framed his text with linguistic and historical annotations that seek to convince us that it is fact. The plot is disarmingly simple: A handsome young Portuguese soldier (Martim Soares Moreno) and Iracema, a beautiful Indian maiden and the virginal priestess of the god Tupã, meet and fall in love – despite differences of race and culture, despite his fealty to the Portuguese crown and her vow of chastity. Iracema's love is deeper and more selfless than that of Martim, and she abandons her tribe and her god to live with him beside the sea. He cannot similarly overcome loyalty and ambition, and leaves her to return to the conquest of Ceará. Iracema gives birth alone to their son, Moacir, and dies of pain and sorrow just as Martim returns. He buries her beside the sea, and sails away with their infant son. Iracema's death is tragic, but it merely reflects the natural and necessary impermanence of existence: "All things upon this earth," Alencar concludes, "must pass" (1967:I, 309).

Iracema appears simple and effortless, and it is difficult not to be so blinded by its charm – in the original or in the graceful nineteenth-century English translation by Isabel Burton (1886) – that we fail to appreciate Alencar's artistry. The novel, upon closer examination, is not simple at all, but functions on three separate levels. The first of these links the work to Alencar's urban novels – in particular to its closest counterpart, *Lucíola*. Like the courtesan, Iracema finds herself forced to go against the most basic moral precepts of her society, to betray her vow of chastity. Iracema's death, like that of Lúcia/Maria, is the inevitable consequence of her sin. She remains pure at heart, however, and that purity and the saving grace of maternity make her an example that ennobles Martim and prepares him for the future.

This, of course, is only one level of Alencar's novel. The story of Martim and Iracema is also a highly symbolic etiology of the creation of Ceará, and of Brazil as a whole. In his *Letters on the Confederation*, Alencar had criticized Gonçalves de Magalhães for failing to include a strong and central female character, suggesting that any truly national poem required an "Indian Eve" as its focus (1960:IV, 878). Iracema is just such a figure, and her love for Martim is thus nothing less than the "American Genesis, a re-creation of Creation," of which Gonçalves Dias had dreamed. *Iracema* is a mythic fusion of opposing natures and cultures, the consummation that Alencar left to the reader's imagination at the end of *The Guarani Indian*. Iracema's function is that of all of the novelist's heroines – to unify and to reconcile, to change and to preserve – on a national scale. She is the New World of the Indian; Martim is white Europe; their child, born of Iracema's suffering and the fruit of her defiance of her god, is a new creation, Brazil itself, both a fusion of Indian and European and the product of the suffering and final destruction of the native world.

Alencar's Garden of Eden on the shores of Ceará gave Brazilians their own creation myth, forming what Antônio Cândido calls "the profound Brazilian desire to perpetuate a [fictional] convention that gives a nation of half-breeds the alibi of a heroic racial past and which provides a young nation with the resonance of a legendary history" (1975:II, 224). But the fusion that takes place in *Iracema* goes beyond the national to the elemental, touching deep and primitive chords. Iracema's name is an anagram of America, the earth itself; she is "the virgin of the forests," the "virgin of the jungle." Martim not only represents war (Mars), but the ocean from which he comes (*mar*, "sea"); he is repeatedly described as "the warrior of the sea."[3]

Land and sea fall in love, but she cannot enter his watery world and he cannot remain amid the hills and forests she represents. The two seek their own Eden – one small area where the Ceará River flows down from the land to meet the sea, a place where the two elements can coexist. The virginal land is made fertile by the water, and a new life is created. But this Eden too must end. The land that gave itself to the sea cannot survive; the sea itself recedes from the short-lived paradise, but takes with it the child – a new creature, our own species: at once earth and water, capable of adapting to both and of dominating both.

In writing *Iracema*, Alencar went beyond all other Indianist writers to create an entirely new style that uses Indian words, and language itself, in daring yet subtle ways. Afrânio Peixoto was the first critic to point out that Iracema's name is an anagram (1931:163), and there are still some modern scholars who refuse to accept the anagram as a conscious creation; they refer to Alencar's insistence, in his notes, that the name combines two Tupi words: *ira* ("honey") and a variant form of *tembe* ("lips") – therefore, "lips of honey" (1967:I, 312). Honey is used in the novel as a symbol of the heroine's sweetness and purity, but Alencar's notes should probably be taken as part of his literary creation, not as the objective annotations of an editor. Similarly, Moacir's name, while a suggestive near-anagram of "Américo," is defined by Alencar's notes as "child of pain," a meaning entirely consonant with Moacir's symbolic function (1967:I, 319).

In reality, as Alencar discovered in the naming of Ceci in *The Guarani Indian*, Tupi phonetics and morphology were so complex, and regional variants so numerous, that almost any combination of letters could be given a suitably symbolic meaning. The same process, moreover, can be seen in my emphasis upon *mar* ("sea") as a component of Martim's name and as a symbolic attribute. It can be argued that Martim Soares Moreno was a real person, one of the leaders in the conquest and settlement of Ceará. Alencar could, nonetheless, have chosen any one of hundreds of other historical figures who participated in events in Brazil. He picked this incident, and structured it in just this way, because he wanted to use every available stylistic and linguistic resource to create his new national mythology. After all, Martim's superior – and a central figure in the conquest and development of Ceará – was Pêro Coelho; his name translates literally as "Peter Rabbit" and just would not have done (Menezes, 1965: 222–4).

Alencar's attention to detail and his stylistic innovations in *Iracema* went far beyond the symbolism of his characters' names. The entirely original language of the novel is another example of his desire and ability to make unifying matches. Over and over, perhaps hundreds of times in this brief work, he makes a statement in standard Portuguese and then, in essence, translates what he has written into a new language; this language is not that spoken by the Tupis, although it contains Indian words. It is, rather, the language of Brazil itself, of the land and its animals and plants, and these similes forge links at once concrete and symbolic between landscape and people, between past and present (Martins Moreira, 1970:123–31).

Iracema, then, is not only the most popular of Alencar's novels; it is also, I believe, a uniquely conscious creation in Brazilian Romanticism, and the sum of the novelist's ideas and goals. In its pages, José de Alencar harmonized the land and the sea, the worlds of the Indian and the white man, the language of men and the language of nature. The heroines of his urban novels had unified society and linked the values of the present to the virtues of the past. Iracema and – to a lesser extent – Cecília unify history and prehistory, joining the race of the present to the race of the past. And, above all, these heroines served to advance Alencar's greatest goal: the creation of a literary tradition that would bond Brazilians both intellectually and emotionally to their own culture and their own land.

Implicit in the conclusions of both *Iracema* and *The Guarani Indian*, however, is another ideological and emotional current, running against the tide of patriotic fervor and evidence of the survival – in Alencar as in other Brazilians – of a very different vision of the nation and its future. Peri and Ceci are swept down the river toward death or toward a new Eden, but also toward the sea, away from the land. In *Iracema*, Moacir is the new creation, Brazil and its people, born of sea and land and of the pain and destruction of the conquest. His Portuguese father, however, carries him away – out to sea, toward Portugal and the racial and cultural unity Portugal represents, toward all the attractions of European culture; we do not know if Moacir will ever find his way home.

4

The poet as slave:
Antônio de Castro Alves

Alencar's sympathetic treatment of the Indian and of Indian–white miscegenation might seem at odds with a political career characterized by vigorous support for the continuation of African slavery in Brazil (Orico, 1977:135-43). In reality, however, Alencar approved of miscegenation only as a historical fact in the distant past and as a metaphor for the formation of a distinctive national character; his speeches suggest that he was particularly fearful of the consequences of any measure weakening the legal and social barriers that separated white Brazilians from the "brutish masses" of blacks and bringing to light the tangled web of illegitimacy, miscegenation, and even incest that characterized the slave system, particularly in rural areas (in Pike, 1969:145–7).

Ironically, the racist attitudes Alencar expressed were almost universally shared by those few white Brazilian writers who actively opposed African slavery – a fact that clearly defines the peculiar and unique character of literary abolitionism in Brazil. The antislavery campaign there began extremely late and produced a scant handful of major works; those works, moreover, rarely made any distinction between attacks on the institution of slavery and attacks on the slaves themselves (Haberly, 1972).

Brazilian abolitionism had barely begun in 1850, when British pressure forced an end to the slave trade. The first description of a slave ship published in Brazil had appeared only six years earlier, a Portuguese translation of a Spanish translation of an English account. This article apparently awakened little sympathy or interest, for no sequels are known to have been printed (Sayers, 1956:71–2). The first and most famous Brazilian poem about a slaver, Castro Alves' "The Slave Ship" ("O Navio Negreiro"), was written in 1868, eighteen years after the actual end of the trade, and was not published in book form until 1880.

The abolition of the Brazilian slave trade made inevitable the eventual disappearance of slavery itself. The institution's survival in Brazil depended upon regular large shipments of able-bodied young African males, and a number of factors – high slave mortality, the scarcity of female slaves, and low slave fertility rates – all presaged abolition by a process of attrition. The only questions, then, were the pace at which abolition was to proceed, and the legal and financial details of the process.[1] Those in favor of rapid and complete abolition sought to convince Brazilians that speed was vitally important, that slavery simply could not be allowed to drag on for three or four generations.

The themes and approaches that had characterized abolitionist campaigns in Europe and North America – appeals to morality and humanitarianism, economic arguments, the standard stereotypes of the Noble African and the Pitiful Slave – seemed too vague, too theoretical, to galvanize the vast majority of national readers to oppose slavery. The Brazilian solution, then, was to insist that African slavery was evil simply because it was directly harmful to whites. The literary campaign against the institution consistently argued that slavery forced white Brazilians into close, daily contact with creatures described as inherently violent and immoral; abolition was the only way to neutralize the physical and moral threat posed by the nation's cruel and vicious chattels.

The force of these antislave appeals can be seen clearly in Joaquim Manuel de Macedo's 1869 *Victims or Executioners? (As Vítimas-Algozes)*, the most exaggerated and sordid product of this antislavery campaign but also one of its most effective efforts. Slavery, Macedo declared in his preface to this collection of short novels, "first affected the slave of our homes and our plantations, the creature who was born human but transformed by captivity into a plague, a wild beast." Macedo warned his readers that "if you consider these narratives carefully, you must abolish slavery, lest they repeat themselves endlessly. For these stories are wholly true, and were and are and shall be so forever – so long as you own slaves. Read, and you shall see" (n.d.:I, xiv–xv). And Brazilians read and believed these tales – of the spoiled houseboy who massacres the master's family; the witch doctor who poisons the livestock, fires the sugarcane, and convinces the cook to seduce the master and poison the mistress and her children; the mulatto maid who teachers her innocent young white charge unspeakable perversions and helps her own lover (a Frenchman, it should be noted, rather than another nonwhite) to seduce the girl, condemning her to a life on the streets.

In all of these abolitionist works, the slave was still a stereotype, a puppet used to call forth powerful emotions of fear and guilt. The black Brazilian was not yet visible as a person, and any possible identification by authors or readers with nonwhite characters was very rare indeed. This barrier between white minds and black emotions was breached only by the greatest antislavery writer Brazil produced, Antônio de Castro Alves.

Castro Alves (1847–71) was born in the interior of Bahia and raised in the provincial capital, Salvador. His parents were prosperous and well connected and planned a legal career for their son. In 1862, when he was fifteen, Castro Alves was sent to study at the prestigious faculty of law in Recife. He failed the entrance exams and enrolled in a cram school, and was not admitted to the law school itself until 1864; he hated his classes there and cut them regularly.

Academic success was unimportant to Castro Alves and his fellow students, in Recife and elsewhere in Brazil. A faculty's primary function was to serve as a holding pen for the nation's future leaders. Largely exempt from external authority, students were allowed and even encouraged to experiment with new ideas and ancient vices, to play at poetry and politics – but always with the clear understanding that these new doctors of law or medicine, having sown all their wild oats, would conform fully to the dictates of family and society.

The rebelliousness of Castro Alves and his friends, then, was largely symbolic and superficial. They smoked and drank too much; they tried, or at least claimed to have tried, opium and hashish; they dressed extravagantly, polished their nails, carmined their lips, and padded their calves. They also chose to be clean-shaven, a great affront to traditional sensibilities; the first beardless actor to appear on a Rio de Janeiro stage had been booed off as blatantly homosexual. These young men also took to parting their hair in the center – a style traditionally used only by women in Brazil. This central part was often widened and shaved clean, and it became so common a form of youthful protest that it was known as the "Road of Liberty" (Haddad, 1953:II, 114–29). Castro Alves was so completely at home within this student world that he never really moved outside its confines. He had managed to get through only three years of law school by the time of his death in 1871, but had accomplished his primary goal – to be idolized by his fellow students both as a poet and as a lover.

Castro Alves began his poetic career in Recife with new versions of the patriotic odes he had declaimed as a boy in Salvador; the easy success of these topical poems encouraged him to view verse as a vehicle for large-scale social change, a medium through which a handful of chosen spirits might express the nation's highest ideals, educate and unify the masses, and alter the course of history. Poetry also served Castro Alves' other ambition: his desire, frankly and rather charmingly expressed, to be a lady-killer. While in Recife, Castro Alves wrote a number of love poems that have since become popular with generations of Brazilian adolescents. Whether declaimed from balconies as homages to actresses or inscribed in the perfumed albums of upper-class maidens, these confident and cheerful expressions of the fantasies of a surprisingly healthy and uncomplicated teenage boy contrast sharply with the frequent allusions to the depression and despair Castro Alves felt were inherent in the poetic vocation (Tolman, 1975).

His most important conquest – and, it would appear, the great love of his short life – ensured Castro Alves' acclamation as the supreme idol of Brazilian students. In 1866 he became the lover of Eugênia Câmara, a well-known Portuguese actress who was touring in Brazil. He was barely nineteen at the time; Eugênia claimed to be around thirty, but a contemporary photograph shows a grim-faced, dumpy, and very plain matron who appears to be at least forty (Leitão de Barros, 1949:72).

Eugênia Câmara was a complex and sophisticated woman who published two volumes of her own verse (Haberly, 1975). She was not a brilliant writer, but she did endeavor, with unique honesty and courage, to describe her life as an actress, set apart from society and from true happiness, using her God-given talent to move audiences but required, in return, to carry out what she called her "sad mission" in life: selling her smiles and tears on the stage, selling her body between performances (Câmara, 1864:47–8). A foreign visitor noted, in 1870, that "an actress who is not a prostitute would be shunned, as unfit for the boards of the theaters" (Codman, 1870:176), and Eugênia and the other leading actresses of the day were expected to be the playthings of wealthy, middle-aged Brazilian men. His fellow students therefore regarded Castro Alves' conquest of Eugênia as a unique generational triumph.

Castro Alves lived with Eugênia for over two years. He wrote a play for her, *Gonzaga*, which they took on tour to Bahia, Rio de Janeiro, and São Paulo; there is some evidence that Castro Alves was accused of pimping for his mistress during this period (Haddad, 1953:I, 73–4). He enrolled in the faculty of law in São Paulo while *Gonzaga* was being readied for presentation there, and once again became the idol of the student population. Eugênia finally tired of Castro Alves in September of 1868, throwing him and his belongings out into the street. One month later, in a curious hunting accident, the young poet discharged his shotgun into his left foot. Gangrene set in, and the shock revived his childhood tuberculosis; the foot was amputated in Rio in 1869, and Castro Alves fled home to Bahia in November of that year.

He returned to his birthplace in the Bahian interior, putting the final touches on his first book of verse, *Floating Foam* (*Espumas Flutuantes*); collecting his abolitionist poems into a second volume, *The Slaves* (*Os Escravos*); and completing a new book, *The Paulo-Afonso Falls* (*A Cachoeira de Paulo Afonso*). Castro Alves moved back to Salvador at the end of September 1870, just in time to see his *Floating Foam* come off the presses, but grew progressively weaker; he died on 6 July 1871, about four months after his twenty-fourth birthday. His many friends vowed to collect money for the posthumous publication of all of his works, but interest flagged; many of the poet's verses did not appear in print until fifty years later (Castro Alves, 1921).

Because Castro Alves is known in Brazil as the "Bard of the Slaves," the great apostle of abolitionism, it is vital to understand the origins of that image and the nature of his commitment to the antislavery movement. He wrote one poem attacking slavery in 1863, when he was sixteen, but he did not genuinely take up the cause until the spring of 1865. He produced at least sixteen abolitionist poems during the next six months or so, but few were published even in student journals (Castro Alves, 1960:819–27). He then turned, rather abruptly, to other interests, and did not return to abolitionism until 1868, when he was in São Paulo. He had decided to publish his antislavery verses as a book, and wrote a friend, "My *Slaves* is almost finished. . . It ends atop the Cubatão mountains [near São Paulo] as dawn is breaking over America, while the morning star – Christ's tear shed for the captives – fades little by little in the west. It is a song of the future. The song of hope" (1960:753).

Few new works were added to the collection after this date, and the poet, preoccupied with his health and with the publication of his largely apolitical *Floating Foam*, did not even mention the abolitionist book in his last letters. Only six of the thirty-four poems now generally accepted as belonging to *The Slaves* appeared, all in periodicals, before Castro Alves' death. About ten of his other abolitionist works were published before the "Golden Law" finally abolished slavery in 1888, but the rest of the collection, half the poems, appear to have remained unknown until 1921 (1960:820–33).

Castro Alves' reputation as the most tireless and influential literary champion of Brazil's slaves may seem somewhat illogical in the face of this chronology. Moreover, few serious efforts have yet been made to understand the origins of his abolitionism. Some critics have been tempted to suggest a geneological explanation; but although Castro Alves' photographs do show quite a swarthy young man, no biographer has been able to come up with any hard evidence of African ancestry.[2] Moreover, Castro Alves' personal life at times contradicted his ideology: For example, his old wet nurse's son, apparently still enslaved, accompanied the young master to Recife and served as his valet.

Why, then, would the scion of a most respectable Bahian family devote his attention to the nation's brutalized and almost invisible slaves? There are, I believe, a number of complementary answers to this vital question. First, the antislavery poems Castro Alves wrote were a vital psychological link to Europe and to European Romanticism. He spent most of his life in small pro-

vincial cities, never managing to take the Grand Tour of the
Continent many of his fellow students in Recife and São Paulo
enjoyed. Through abolitionism, however, he could define himself as a distant American cousin of the greatest European intellectuals, submerging the specific, local problem of Brazilian slavery
within the broader context of what he saw as the universal struggle of liberalism against tyranny and oppression. Castro Alves
thus equated his own efforts with those of Byron, Mickiewicz,
Kossuth, and Hugo (1960:211–14). This contextual diffusion weakened the force of Castro Alves' abolitionism, which was always
philosophical rather than political in nature, but it did allow him
to portray himself as a gallant champion of freedom – a vague
ideal with which few could disagree – and only secondarily as an
advocate of the abolition of slavery in Brazil, a position that was
both more dangerous and less immediately popular.

A second reason was that fidelity to a great and noble cause,
like freedom, appeared to be an integral part of the image of the
true poet. And although Castro Alves seems to have believed, in
a very general way, in the inevitability of technical and moral
progress in the "century of light," he simultaneously implied
that the noble cause was most valid, at least as a poetic attribute,
when it failed. This contradiction was merely one component in
a set of balanced contradictions that lay at the heart of his vision
of the natural and social order, and of the role of the poet within
that order. His cosmology and ideology, it should be stressed,
were not at all original; they were clearly rooted in European
Romanticism. But certain aspects of that Romantic tradition, particularly the implicit tendency toward self-destruction, appear to
have been intensified by the hothouse isolation of nineteenth-
century Brazil.

The universe, for Castro Alves, was a series of antitheses:
"Every nighttime – has its dawning, / Rays of light for every
darkness" (1960:212). This opposition was paralleled, in human
terms, by the equally eternal conflicts between good and evil,
joy and sorrow, wealth and poverty, and so on. It was the
responsibility of the superior being Castro Alves classified as the

Genius to live within the context of these contradictions, and to make them clear to lesser mortals. Castro Alves recognized two special categories of genius, the poet and the artist; he identified himself as a genius, and as both poet and artist.

The essential unity of poet and artist can help us to understand Castro Alves' ideology, his vocation, and his function. As we shall see, that unity was also fundamental to the poetic expression of his ideas. Artists, for Castro Alves, were above all actors and actresses; they could mirror extremes of emotion, assume morally divergent roles, and personify for their audiences the ideological and ethical conflicts dramatists created. This ability, and the fame it might bring, not only were balanced by the social and moral marginality of an artist like Eugênia Câmara, but in fact depended upon it. The blasphemous poem Castro Alves declaimed to Eugênia after she had been booed by an audience in Recife is the most extreme exposition of this theory:

> We come together now but to adore you;
> You are all our glory, all our faith.
> We rise in pride if we but fall before you;
> Humbled at your feet, ourselves we raise!...
>
> .   .   .
>
> Great as only genius can be great,
> You are as brilliant as the very light;
> Before the mob – art's Calvary of hate –
> The stage became your cross, and you were Christ!...[3]

The poet was simply the artist writ large; the poetic life was a performance, and verse but one aspect of that performance. The poet had to embody the extremes of existence as a precondition to their expression – to be, in Castro Alves' phrase, both "genius and beggar" (1960:130). This vision of the poet's role was, at least initially, a pose adopted by an ambitious and basically cheerful teenager. One of the most charming aspects of Castro Alves' lyrics is his often lighthearted, self-mocking awareness of the pose and of its utility in attracting women. "God made the snow – for the dark mountain peak," he wrote to one girl; "God made the maiden – for the lonely Bard" (1960:109).

The tragic mask of the poet, the "Don Juan of death" (1960:108), was also an expression of Castro Alves' rejection of what he and other students considered the pettiness and banality of upper-class life in imperial Brazil. His family wanted a successful young lawyer; he would cut classes to devote himself to wine, women, and song. Amid the technological progress and political stability of Pedro II's Empire, Castro Alves longed for military glory and espoused a nebulous ideology of republicanism and naive social-ism. "The square belongs to the people," he declared, "as the sky belongs to the condor" (1960:432). The people to whom Castro Alves referred, however, were not the vulgar masses; he meant, instead, that the civil authorities of Recife should not interfere with the freedom of movement and action of the faculty's students.

If abolitionism, at the beginning, was both the noble cause of the true poet and one symptom of Castro Alves' general rebel-lion against the world outside the faculty, it was to become far more important to him than he had envisioned. The role of the poet satisfied all of his short-term ambitions – fame, the love of an actress, acclaim as a Student Prince – but his poems and his correspondence contain almost no trace of any vision of a more distant future, beyond the limits of his drawn-out adolescence. There are no hints of any ability to see past these youthful goals or to convert them into concrete achievements. We find, instead, a young man increasingly caught up in the pose he had adopted, becoming genuinely desperate and frustrated. Castro Alves could accept, as an intellectual proposition, the Romantic axiom that poetic glory had to be balanced by the failure of the noble cause, by physical suffering, and, in the end, by an early death – the ultimate proof of his identity as a poet, the only identity he possessed. To accept this destiny literally was far more difficult. Castro Alves had created the role of poet for himself, playing it with enormous success up and down Brazil; ultimately, he saw no way to escape from an identity that had become as much a prison as the bourgeois future of family and professional obliga-tions against which he had originally rebelled.

It was this sense of oppression and entrapment – first by society, but ultimately by the poetic pose itself – that was the primary basis for Castro Alves' abolitionism. What set him apart from other white Brazilians of his generation was his deep, personal identification with the nation's slaves – "the captives," as he generally referred to them. Their color was relatively unimportant to Castro Alves; he utilized it only within the context of the universal antithesis of light and darkness. Because darkness might symbolize evil, however, he also felt free, when necessary, to whiten his slaves and darken their oppressors: Some of his slave characters are very light-skinned, even "pallid," and those whites who torment them are swarthy or deeply tanned by the sun (1960:287; 230, 278).

Race was almost as unimportant as color. The African origin of the nation's slaves merely established their symbolic value – the children of Ham and of Hagar, forever in bondage. For Castro Alves, their captivity, ordained by history and geography, was as inevitable as his own entrapment by society and by the poetic destiny. In terms of the Brazilian model of racial categories, then, it is clear that for Castro Alves one element in the social component of the continuum as it existed in his time, lack of freedom, was so acute in his own case that it moved him down the scale toward blackness, toward an almost absolute psychological identification with the slaves.

This basic fact – that Castro Alves was writing not about the slaves but about himself – explains the nature of his abolitionism. Slavery was a personal metaphor, and his inability to formulate a political program that would lead to abolition simply reflected his acceptance of the inevitability of his own captivity. He did not expect Brazil to abolish slavery, at least in the near future, because he saw no viable solution to the crisis of his own life.

Modern critics have often been perplexed by Castro Alves' most famous abolitionist poem, "The Slave Ship," written in São Paulo in April of 1868; in that work, he vehemently demanded that Brazil put an end to the slave trade – a step that British pressure had forced the Empire to take some eighteen years before. "The Slave Ship" is an anacronism, however, only if we insist upon viewing the poet's abolitionism as political rather than philosophical and psychological. In reality, in this poem as in his other major abolitionist works, Castro Alves was endeavoring to create metaphoric structures, based upon the traditions of Brazilian Romanticism, which would allow him to describe the effects of his own captivity.

The focus of these structures is a series of literary commonplaces, the standard psychological refuges of despairing poets: Brazil itself, the ideal of innocence and natural beauty, its lush vastness a metaphor for absolute freedom from constraint; the childhood home, emblem of purity and maternal love and protection; the sea, symbolic of escape and of boundless liberty; and the interior of Brazil, specifically the landscape around his birthplace, which for Castro Alves combined natural beauty, physical and emotional freedom, and the pure joy of childhood.

In his major antislavery works, Castro Alves methodically described the progressive contamination and destruction of these places of refuge by slavery. This process of gradually intensifying entrapment paralleled and symbolized the erosion of options for escape in his own life. Slavery, first, is alien to the purity of America; it was brought by Europe, "the great whore" (1960:291). The institution, "a noisome crocodile / Cast from the darkling waves of the Nile / To take its refuge here" has forever stained the Brazilian landscape; the palm trees of Gonçalves Dias now "twist in torment / When they hear... / The cry of pain" (1960:216–17). Even the wild condor, Castro Alves' ultimate symbol of the freedom from constraint possible in the New World, "has become the vulture, / The bird of enslavement" (1960:293).

Slavery also infects and destroys the refuge of family life in "Tragedy on the Hearth" ("Tragédia no Lar"), in which a slave mother goes insane with grief and rage when her infant child is taken from her to be sold (1960;229–35). "The Slave Ship" was probably written to complement this poem; its original title, retained as the subtitle, was "Tragedy at Sea" ("Tragédia no Mar") (Haddad, 1953:II, 105). The two works, moreover, are very similar in their description of the triumph of evil and constraint over the forces of love and freedom. The "Dantean nightmare" of the slave ship turns both captives and keepers into demonic beasts, pollutes both sky and ocean with its horror, and stains the once-proud Brazilian flag, which flies above the ship, transforming it into a shroud (1960:277–84).

Castro Alves' most ambitious abolitionist work, the long dramatic poem *The Paulo-Afonso Falls*, was completed in 1870. Portions of it appear to have been written earlier, however, for Castro Alves read parts of it aloud to José de Alencar in 1868 (Menezes, 1965:233). The poem glorifies the interior of Bahia, "the nesting-place of the poet" (1960:100). The two slaves who inhabit that landscape, Maria and Lucas, owe a great deal to Alencar's Indians. Like Iracema and Peri, Maria and Lucas are part of the land and are therefore utterly pure and beautiful. Their natural happiness is destroyed by the personal consequences of slavery: Maria is raped by the white son of their master, and the violence of this crime, symbolic of the slave system as a whole, transforms the peaceful landscape of the interior into a series of images of bestial brutality (Gomes, 1953:41–2).

Lucas longs for vengeance, but Castro Alvers stays his hand; the noble slave, like the poet himself, is an emblem of suffering rather than a man of action. In a contrived flashback, we learn that the rapist is really Lucas' half-brother, and that Lucas long ago promised his dying mother that he would never harm any member of their master's family. There can be no escape for Lucas and Maria except death; in a replication of the famous ending of *The Guarani Indian*, the couple's fragile canoe takes them over the falls. Alencar carefully left his readers two options for Peri and Ceci: union only after death, or the terrestrial consummation of their love and the mythic creation of a new race. For Castro Alves, however, the death of his characters is the inescapable precondition for happiness and freedom; all of nature unites to perform a ritual that is both wedding and funeral:

> Let the waves, like fair virgins, part
> That the Bride may pass!...

> "The stars above twinkle! – As torches!
> The cliffs murmur low!... – As monks!
>   An organ prays in the sky!
> For incense! – the doves rise from the depths!
> For censer – the Paulo-Afonso Falls!
> The priest! – is God Himself..."[4]

Thus the final refuge, for Castro Alves as for his slave characters, was the liberation of death. The equation of freedom and the grave explains Castro Alves' inability to see abolitionism as a political cause; it must, as well, have made his poems against slavery far more palatable and less threatening to white audiences. Despite his sincerity and his identification with the captives, his abolitionist verses were not calls to action, but appeals for pity and paeans to resignation.

Castro Alves' contemporaries also must have found it difficult to separate his message from its medium – the poet's flamboyant and charismatic recitation of verses written to be declaimed in public and only rarely set down in print. He appeared before his audiences, Joaquim Nabuco recalled, "dressed in black in order to give a touch of sadness to his features; his brow furrowed, as if his thoughts weighed heavily upon him; his eyes, deep and luminous, fixed on a point in space; his lips slightly drawn back in scorn, or open in a smile of triumph" (in Peixoto, 1976:19). Moreover, "everyone who heard him got goosepimples of astonishment," and saw him as "more demigod than poet, less poet than prophet" (Peixoto, 1976:20). In São Paulo, "shouts, delirium, cheers, frenzy – such was the overwhelming reaction to every line; every idea, every thought caused a sensation in the audience" (in Calmon, 1973:197).

The written record – Castro Alves' published poems – is an imperfect substitute for an experience that cannot be re-created. His verses, like those of many of his contemporaries, are filled with the peculiar typographical residue of oral recitation: forests of exclamation points and question marks that denote verbal flourishes we cannot hear, dramatic gestures we cannot see; dashes that represent sudden and theatrical shifts in pitch and volume; ellipses that are the last trace of dying voices long since dead.

Our appreciation of Castro Alves' poetry is distorted as well by the gulf between our expectations and those of his audience. Ruth Finnegan has noted that a fundamental characteristic of oral poetry – and Castro Alves was above all an oral poet – is the impact upon form and content of the immediate and constant interplay between the creator-reciter and the needs and feelings of the audience (1977:88–90, 214–43). In order to understand the poetry of Castro Alves within this oral context, therefore, it is important to define those needs and expectations. His contemporaries, first, wanted spontaneity: Improvisation, whether real or feigned with the help of a good memory, was almost a religious experience for an audience, privileged to witness this brief moment of contact between the ether of divine aspiration and the genius of the poet. Innovation was very difficult, given the strictures of this demand for spontaneity, and poets tended to draw upon a common pool of set words and images familiar to them and to their listeners – a process similar to the Parry-Lord theory of oral composition within the Homeric tradition. As a result, the poets of Castro Alves' generation often independently produced almost identical phrases (F. Cunha, 1971:81–105).

In addition to spontaneity, audiences wanted to experience what can best be described as the interplay of sensations; they did not seek complex and profound ideas or emotions, nor could they have appreciated such elements within the context of a brief oral performance. The poet's goal was to use language to encode sensations, to transmit a sense of pain or a sense of joy, for example, to his audience. This poetry of sensations was most effective, and most faithful to the Romantic cosmology of antithesis, when equally strong but very different sensations were juxtaposed. The ultimate catharsis for an audience – and one which contemporary accounts make it clear that Castro Alves' verbal talent, charismatic presence, and theatrical flair often provided – was to experience such rapid and absolute shifts in sensation that all the circuits blew in a mass ecstasy of shouts and fainting spells.

One of the poet's standard devices in pursuit of this goal was rhetorical antithesis; Castro Alves often abused this sort of simplistic pairing of antagonic encoded sensations, like joy and sorrow, hope and despair, but the effect must still have been very impressive when complemented by the oratorical pauses and changes in posture, facial expression, and voice tone that we see recorded only as dashes. A good example of this technique appears in Castro Alves' description of the martyred missionaries of colonial Brazil:

> "Pain, – you are pleasure!
> The rack, – but a bed! Hot irons, – shining jewels!
> The stake, – is a sceptor! The fire, – but a gem!
> Oh death, – you are life!"[5]

Castro Alves, however, also encoded more complex and subtle sensations, involving spatial relationships as well as emotions. This process can be seen, for example, in a poem improvised in October of 1870. After listening to several other poets recite their works, Castro Alves rose to salute their efforts:

> Sometimes the shepherd climbing up the Alps
> Casts down his tremulous song into the abyss.
> The bottomless depths beneath – reply below!
> The heavens of infinite size – reply above!
>
> Poet! The voice of the wandering herdsman there
> Echoed within your soul… It rose!… It grew!
> Your soul is deep – deep as the chasm is deep!
> Your genius is lofty – lofty as is the sky![6]

Castro Alves here had a single commonplace idea – the universality of the poet, encompassing the opposed absolutes of depth and height – and a single, banal image – the shepherd's yodel, echoing through the Alps. The key to the poem's effectiveness as oral poetry however, is neither the idea nor the image, but the rapid juxtaposition and alternation of sensations of height and depth. The recitation of these lines, augmented by theatrical gestures and by rising and falling intonation, might well have induced vertigo in particularly sensitive listeners.

This interplay of spatial sensations, in a far more sophisticated form, is a basic stylistic element in Castro Alves' greatest poems – in the first five stanzas of "The Slave Ship," for example:

> We are at sea... And wildly, there in space,
> A gilded butterfly – the moon – cavorts,
> And after it the waves first run... then stop
> Like restless groups of children at their play.
>
> We are at sea... And from the firmament
> The stars leap down like bits of golden froth...
> The sea replies by lighting secret fires –
> The constellations of its liquid wealth...
>
> We are at sea... And two infinities
> There come together in a mad embrace;
> Cerulean, golden, placid or sublime...
> Which of the two is heaven? Which the sea?...
>
> We are at sea... And opening her sails
> To the hot and panting breath of ocean winds,
> The masted brig goes skimming through the waves,
> A swallow swooping down to touch the foam.
>
> Her home?... Her destination?... Who can tell
> For wandering ships when oceans are so vast?
> In this Saharan desert, steeds raise dust
> And gallop swift, but never leave a trace.[7]

In these stanzas, Castro Alves is balancing antithetical spatial sensations that would have been greatly intensified in his public performances of "The Slave Ship." The central message of the poem is very simple indeed: Freedom is good; lack of freedom is bad. The poet communicates that message, in part, through a series of rapid shifts from stasis to movement. The phrase "We are at sea" does not fully translate the Portuguese " 'Stamos em pleno mar," which better conveys a sensation of isolation and of immobility, one pole of the implicit antithesis. The other pole, in the horizontal plane, is the expansive freedom of movement of the waves, the wind, the ship itself, and the African horses; this last element sets up a parallel contrast, later in the poem, between the lost freedom of Africa and the present captivity of the slaves in the ship's hold.

Stasis and motion also alternate rapidly in the vertical plane, as they do in the improvisation cited previously; the stability of the ship, delicately balanced between sea and sky, is set against extreme, free-ranging movement between these "two infinities." This vertical antithesis is also reinforced in the next sections of the poem by the contrast between the surface of the deck – the world of the sailors, archetypes of man's freedom to roam as he wishes – and the "Dantean nightmare" of the fettered world beneath it. By the conclusion of "The Slave Ship," the crime of slavery has polluted the sea, the sky, and Brazil itself – an equally potent symbol of vastness and freedom. The captivity of the slaves, and of their poet, forces a halt to all movement: "Columbus," Castro Alves demands, "shut up the gateways to your seas!" (1960:284)

This fragmentary analysis of the spatial sensations Castro Alves encoded and juxtaposed in "The Slave Ship" shows his enormous technical virtuosity within this oral, largely nonintellectual style. It also underscores, however, the practical futility of much of his abolitionist verse. His audiences were moved to shouts or tears, but these poems did not really touch their deepest emotions or their intellects. Once their nerve-endings stopped tingling, Castro Alves' listeners perhaps recalled only the nebulous platitudes that all of his artistry was designed to convey.

It might seem, then, that Castro Alves, despite his talent and his unique ability to identify with the nation's black slaves, failed in his mission. Ironically, however, the poet's basic assumptions turned out to be correct: Symbol was in fact more important than substance, and the verses the true poet produced were but one aspect of his most sublime creation – the poetic life and its necessary corollary, the poetic death. Most of Castro Alves' poems remained unpublished, but when abolitionism finally developed as a political force in the decades following his death, his image provided a suitably heroic focus for the campaign – the image of the tragic young genius who had, in some vague and totally unexplained fashion, sacrificed his life for the slaves. Castro Alves' apotheosis as nothing less than the "Christ of the Slaves" helped make abolitionism respectable for white Brazilians in the eighties, and contributed to the final victory of the cause. And although his abolitionism may now appear overly personal and passive, Castro Alves' vision of himself as a captive, expressed through the sympathetic black characters he created, finally made black Brazilians equal members of the racial trinity, symbols of the nation and of its sadness as valid as the Indians.

The sense of sadness, loss and alienated entrapment that enabled Castro Alves to identify with the slaves also reinforced the themes of exile and of unworthiness we have seen in colonial writers and in Gonçalves Dias. What is new, in the verse of Castro Alves, is the systematic negation of the traditional poetic options for escape – the ideal of Brazil, the innocence and beauty of the land and of its primitive inhabitants, the happy memories of childhood. Even the ultimate refuge – the sea, symbolic of a return of to the less complex and tragic Portuguese identity – is destroyed in "The Slave Ship." Castro Alves' successors were thus compelled to abandon these simple visions of re-creation and reintegration, and to seek personal and national identity within the new world of urban Brazil, and within themselves.

5

A journey through the escape hatch: Joaquim Maria Machado de Assis

It is difficult indeed to summarize and characterize the life and works of Joaquim Maria Machado de Assis (1839–1908), Brazil's greatest writer and the most original novelist to appear in the Western Hemisphere in the nineteenth century; such are the ironies and ambiguities of Machado's ideas about life and about literature, and the self-deprecating, reader-mocking subtleties of his style. Critics have inevitably tended to focus upon the search for constants and certainties in a literary career that lasted for more than half a century. But Machado never claimed to be consistent; the unreliability of the narrative voice – in his first-person novels and, even more remarkably, in the third-person *Quincas Borba* – is one of the hallmarks of his fiction. His works, in fact, make clear his extreme distrust of all unitary explanations of human character and behavior.

One fundamental problem, with which all of Machado's critics and biographers have wrestled, is the relationship between Machado the man and Machado the author. Some scholars have respected the novelist's public insistence that his works were entirely independent of his life; other critics, frustrated and fascinated by the enormous lacunae in our knowledge of Machado's personal life, have viewed all of his works as detailed autobiographies. I believe that it is possible to strike some sort of balance between these two critical traditions – to recognize the universality of the basic human problems that Machado treated in his fiction, while seeking to understand how his life and his society helped form Machado's consciousness of those problems.

It is symptomatic of the uncertainty and controversy that surround Machado that even the most basic of facts, his racial identity, remains the subject of an often heated debate. Our concrete knowledge of Machado's ancestry can be briefly summarized: Both his paternal great-grandmothers appear to have been black slaves; at least one paternal great-grandfather was white, possibly a priest. Machado's paternal grandparents were legally defined as free and brown-skinned (*pardos*), but one effect of the social component of racial identity in Brazil was the classification of slaves as black (*prêtos*) and freedmen as *pardos*, independent of their ancestry or somatology. His father was a free artisan attached to a wealthy white family whose lands covered much of Livramento Hill, overlooking Rio de Janeiro's harbor. Machado's mother was a white woman born in the Azores and, most probably, brought to Brazil as a child. She was at least minimally literate, and worked for the same noble family; it appears likely that she served as a lady's maid and companion. Machado's mother died of tuberculosis in 1849, and his father married a mulatto woman, Maria Inês, in 1854 (Massa, 1971:32–72).

This is about all we really know about Machado's ancestry and his childhood; the rest is speculation. His contemporaries frequently noted his careful and consistent refinement, and it seems probable that Machado acquired this refinement on Livramento Hill, protected and encouraged by the owner of the estate and by her family. The boy learned to read and write and somewhere picked up a knowledge of French, so essential for social and intellectual acceptance; by 1859, when he was twenty, Machado could write poetry in French (Massa, 1971:74–8).

Machado's intelligence and his learning prepared him to rise above his parents' social status, and opened up occupations best described as educated manual labor: clerk, bookkeeper, typesetter, or proofreader. He may well have tried his hand at several such jobs when he became independent of his father, sometime around the age of fifteen. By 1859 Machado had found a new patron, Francisco de Paula Brito, an influential mulatto printer and publisher; it was around the same time that Machado began to produce his first literary texts. From then on, his intense ambition and his literary and social talents moved him slowly but inexorably toward heights his family could scarcely have imagined: renown as a writer and critic; friendship with the best and the brightest of his generation; marriage to a white Portuguese woman of good family; important positions in the bureaucracy; and the presidency of the Brazilian Academy of Letters.

In 1859, however, Machado de Assis did not seem destined for such greatness. Physically, he appeared frail; he was extremely nearsighted; he stuttered. Late in life he suffered frequent and severe attacks of epilepsy, and it is likely that some symptoms appeared during his youth. And – the most important element in this catalogue of social and physical handicaps that late nineteenth-century Brazilians would have defined as *taras*, or hereditary defects – Machado was not white.

How black was Machado de Assis? The only honest answer is that we really do not know, since racial identity in Brazil is so variable, so much a function of nongenetic, nonsomatic elements. The early photographs of the novelist show a very dark young man, with traits that surely would have been perceived as clear evidence of African ancestry: lightly-kinked hair, a thick lower lip, and a broad and flat nose (*Revista do Livro*, 1958:226–7). The social component of the racial continuum, however, allowed Machado de Assis – refined, well-dressed, surrounded and protected by influential friends – to be perceived as light-skinned. It even enabled many of his contemporaries to ignore the somatic evidence altogether and to accept him as entirely white and European. Writing after Machado's death, José Veríssimo described him as a "mulatto, [who] was in reality a Greek of the greatest [*i.e.*, classical] period" (David, 1957:155). One of the novelist's friends, the distinguished statesman Joaquim Nabuco, wrote Veríssimo to complain:

I would not have called Machado a *mulatto*, and I believe that nothing would hurt him more than this classification. . . Machado was white to me, and I think he thought of himself in the same way: whatever alien blood there might have been [in his veins], it in no way affected his purely Caucasian character. I, at least, saw in him only the Greek. [David, 1957:164]

The most reasonable approach to the question of Machado's race, I believe, is simply to accept the impossibility of any single classification. As a boy and as a young man, it seems highly unlikely that Machado was unaware of his African ancestry and its social implications; he was, after all, only a bit more than two generations away from the slave quarters. He learned, while still very young, that certain behavior patterns could counteract or at least attenuate the prejudice his appearance might awaken. So he struggled to improve himself – to dress well; to know the right people; to speak and write correctly; to learn more foreign languages than his white friends, and to know them better. He was determined to appear immensely learned in both classical and modern literature, to shun confession and controversy at all cost, and to avoid personal slurs by gently poking fun at himself first.

It is clear that Machado's refinement, the product of this struggle, led many of his friends and associates to perceive him as at or very near the white end of the racial continuum; it is probable that their support and acceptance allowed Machado to think of himself as white, perhaps much of the time. It is also true, however, that this whiteness was situational rather than intrinsic, and it is illogical to suggest that Machado did not occasionally find himself in situations in which his somatology was more visible than his culture, in which he was treated, even if only momentarily, as a nonwhite.

Though it is important to avoid falling into the autobiographical trap, pursuing one-on-one correlations between life and work, Machado's isolated and fundamentally vulnerable existence on the other side of the mulatto escape hatch inevitably influenced his ideas and his writing. His works can be seen as a highly evasive and ambiguous journal of his passage from nonwhiteness to whiteness, a journal that focuses upon three central problems: the nature of identity, the nature of time, and the character and meaning of the transformations in identity that occur as an individual moves through time and through society.

Machado de Assis wrote that he was suckled, as a young man, on "pure Romantic milk" (1962:III, 810), and the general themes of Brazilian Romanticism can be found throughout his superficially anti-Romantic work. The emphasis upon antithesis, deeply embedded in the lives and verses of Castro Alves and his generation, appears in Machado's works as well – not only in his early poetry, but also in his mature fiction. Although his view of the essential bifurcation of life was both more complex and more psychological than that of the Romantics, Machado similarly defined every individual as a binomial, and explored the symbiotic relationship between these two distinct identities.

The first of these, the internal identity, is the essence of the being at birth, its original natural (that is, physical) and social condition. It was inevitable that Machado, born socially dependent, physically frail, and nonwhite, should have meditated at length upon the meaning of the vast disparities that exist in nature's creations. Braz Cubas, in his *Posthumous Memoirs (Memórias Póstumas de Braz Cubas)*, ponders a few of the many examples of such disparities that exist in Machado's fiction: Eugênia, born beautiful but crippled; Prudência, doomed to a miserable and utterly meaningless existence; the black butterfly Braz kills, but would have spared had it been blue. Despite all his efforts to use fictional characters and situations as a means of clarifying and rationalizing these disparities in origin, Machado finds no solution; our beginnings, the internal identities that we retain forever, are the result of pure chance (the lottery in *Dom Casmurro*) or of the equally aleatory egotism and occasional bad taste of Nature-Pandora as she appears to Braz Cubas (1962:I, 518–22).

If the internal identity is both incomprehensible and beyond our control, like Machado's ancestry and his physical defects, the external identity – our image in the mirror the world holds up to us; not what we are but what we are perceived to be – would seem to be social rather than natural, learned rather than genetic. To Machado, however, the social imperatives of the external identity – to be respected and loved, to rise to the limits of ambition, to feel superior to all those around us – appeared as irrational and as inescapable as the laws or whims of nature (Faoro, 1974:335).

Ideally, the external identity should conform exactly to the contours of the internal self in a balanced symbiosis, defining it and protecting it – like a uniform, in "The Mirror" ("O Espelho"), Machado's most complete exposition of the two selves and their relationship (1962:II, 345–52); like a well-fitted glove; like Braz Cubas' medicinal plaster for the soul (1962:I, 512–13).[1] Such balance and conformity, however, is almost always as illusory as Braz Cubas' miraculous medical discovery, and the few cases Machado does present create other problems – for his characters as well as for us, the readers. In "The Secret Cause" ("A Causa Secreta"), Fortunato is the truly happy man; he has managed to structure his external self – his career as a nurse, his many good deeds and his consequent fame as a humanitarian, even his choice of a wife and of a best friend and partner – so that it perfectly conforms to his internal identity. The most fundamental characteristic of that internal identity, however, is a terrifying sadism that feeds hungrily on the suffering of others (1962:II, 511–19).

In general, however, Machado's characters are not as congruent as Fortunato; the external identity contradicts or dwarfs the internal self, creating a destructive, antipathetic symbiosis. The effects of such imbalance are sometimes hilarious, sometimes tragic, but always ironic. In the most extreme cases of discontinuity, moreover, individuals whose own identities fail to satisfy their needs form fragile and mutually parasitic relationships with others, relationships that lead inevitably to exploitation and betrayal.[2]

The complex and problematic symbiosis of the double self, however, is not static, but moves through time. Machado's use of fictive time is astonishingly modern. It is quite distinct from chronological time, and its perceived velocity – the duration of events within the text – depends upon the importance of those events, how much they alter characters or situations. More fundamental than the velocity of time and of the changes it brings is its direction, a problem Machado raises again and again. Is time cyclical, repetitive, and therefore susceptible of some rational organization; or is it linear and infinite and irrational? Can it be described as a circle – for Ezequiel Maya the first and most basic of human abstractions (1962:II, 925)? Or is time a series of unconnected words, each written down, erased, and then replaced by another (1962:II, 570)? If time is cyclical, the changes that it measures can be arranged, understood, perhaps even predicted. If time is linear and particulate, then even the most fundamental events in an individual's life are disconnected, irrational, and ultimately meaningless.

Machado's most coherent yet pessimistic response to these problems appears in Braz Cubas' delirium (1962:I, 518–22). The existence of individuals and of humanity itself, as Pandora presents it to Braz, fuses both possible visions of time and of change:

There are real or apparent cycles – birth and death, the rise and fall of people and of nations – but the whole sweep of past, present, and future is terrifying in its immensity and maddening in its utter meaninglessness. The best revenge is not to live well, but to deny Pandora the pleasure of creating and destroying yet another plaything – to follow Braz Cubas' example: "I had no children; I did not pass on to any other being the legacy of our human misery" (1962:I, 637).

This vision, while the most extreme, is not Machado's only approach to the problem of metaempirical change. In his fiction, the passage of time brings with it two orders of transformations, natural and social. There are, first, the changes that affect the internal identity: A child is born, grows up, ages, and dies. These transformations of the inner, physical self as it moves through time may be difficult to face, but they are at least regular, predictable, and universal. The second set of changes transforms the external self and is far more difficult for the individual to come to terms with and to understand.

As an individual moves through society, the inescapable dictates of ambition require a series of metamorphoses of the external self; such transformations are contingent upon hard choices between the imperatives of the external identity and the basic morality – often described by Machado in nonmoral terms as simple pride – of the inner self. In Machado's works, the needs of the mirror-self almost invariably triumph, destroying the ideal balance of the two symbiotic identities. What we call society, in fact, is for Machado no more than the sum of an infinite number of immoral or amoral interactions. Every external self strives endlessly to assert, improve, or protect itself at the expense of others, a process Machado describes in terms of rolling balls that clack into one another, transferring their kinetic energy in a series of random reactions (1962:I, 558). The inner self demands an accounting, however, and the two identities can only be reintegrated if the external self can order and justify its actions and its metamorphoses as both rational and inevitable.

Machado, it is true, was not the first writer to recognize the gap between what we are and what we appear to be, between self and image; it seems equally true, however, that his obsession with the double self was firmly rooted in his awareness of his own situation as a nonwhite who had managed to move his perceived identity to the white extreme of the racial continuum, but who could not escape the remnants of his past. Similarly, although the conflict between morality and ambition is a universal theme, that conflict must have often been acute as Machado himself passed through the escape hatch. He simply could not have moved so successfully along the continuum had he not sacrificed conscience to ambition in several fundamental areas: He separated himself from his family; he turned his back on other nonwhite intellectuals; and he refused to use his prestige, at least publicly, to advance the abolitionist cause.[3]

In his works, Machado tried hard to rationalize the choices of his own life, to remove them from the area of morality and individual responsibility. He toyed with – and, I believe, finally rejected – three deterministic theories that might appear to justify the actions of the external self: physiology, psychiatry, and sociology. Machado disposed of the belief that human behavior is entirely a function of physiology, and therefore both inevitable and predictable, in one of his most grotesque and bitter stories, "Alexandrine Tale" ("Conto Alexandrino"). The ancient doctors who seek internal physical evidence of evil are far more criminally unbalanced than the criminals they dissect alive, piece by piece; their science is no more than the expression of their own ambition for success (1962:II, 411–17).

Psychiatry meets a similar fate at Machado's hands. He is tempted to believe that everyone is mad, to one degree or another, and that this universal dementia explains and excuses human immorality and amorality; psychiatry, however, turns out to be but another manifestation of insanity. In "The Psychiatrist" ("O Alienista"), Dr. Simão Bacamarte at first cures those who appear mad by catering to the irrational ambitions of their external selves, without seeking to address the causes of the imbalance between the two identities. The psychiatrist finally concludes, however, that he alone is mad and therefore should be the sole inhabitant of his vast asylum, which has taken over an entire town. This is not a revolutionary new theory of psychiatry; it merely expresses the final triumph of the obsessive desire of the doctor's external self to be superior and unique, to set himself apart from others if only by madness (1962:II, 253–88).

The rationalization Machado found most appealing was deterministic sociology, the complex of ideas borrowed from Comte, Spencer, and the Social Darwinists that Machado called "Humanitism." He wanted desperately to believe that the imperatives of the external self are both morally defensible and paramount; that the potatoes, in the parable he presents in *Quincas Borba*, belong by right to the winners who obey those imperatives; that there are really no losers in the struggle, since life's victims are simply reabsorbed into the life-force (1962:I, 644–7). Nevertheless, Machado rejected this theory because it was too facile and, perhaps, because social determinism was so often used by his white contemporaries to explain and to justify the inferior status of Brazil's nonwhites.

Quincas Borba documents Machado's rejection of Humanitism. What defeats the theory is not its ridiculous exaggerations or the obvious insanity of its chief proponent, but, rather, the novel itself as Machado structured it. That structure juxtaposes two separate texts: the theory of Humanitism and a narrative that purports to prove the theory's validity. The narrative makes it clear, however, that life has no winners – with the possible exception of the dog, who is not even part of the game. And although the theory asserts that we should not care what happens to those, like Rubião, who appear to lose, the entire narrative is designed to touch the emotions and morality of our inner selves, to make us identify with Rubião through the utter pathos of his betrayal, insanity, and death. Machado does not suggest an alternative explanation for human behavior, but simply forces the problem back upon us as his readers.

If the actions of the external self cannot be justified, the transformations through which it passes must, at least, be ordered and studied; only in this way can the individual perceive and understand the origins and the consequences of change. This process requires the creation and utilization of texts – a word here used in a very broad sense – which are concrete expressions of the external self at certain moments in its life. Through the juxtaposition and comparison of such texts, Machado's characters seek, however ridiculously or tragically, to order change, to make it meaningful. In extreme cases, these same texts are used to negate time and to deny change.

One set of texts, for Machado and his characters, is formed of the artifacts that define the external identity: houses, clothes, means of transportation, furniture – even tombstones and coffins. The young lieutenant's uniform, in "The Mirror," is an artifactual text. So is Bento Santiago's childhood home in *Dom Casmurro*; and Bento's painstaking reconstruction of that house is the key to his need to find meaning in the events of his life (1962:I, 807–9). Other texts are the spouses, lovers, and friends Machado's characters choose, but these ambiguous and unreliable living texts are themselves torn between the two identities as they pass through their own series of transformations. The most problematic of all human texts are children, who may or may not, as Pandora's whims decree, reflect the identities of their parents.[4]

The names Machado chose for his characters provide yet another set of texts, sometimes straightforward, sometimes playful, sometimes devilishly ironic (Caldwell, 1960:32–61). Family names and given names would seem to reflect the original self before its passage through time and society. Names change, however, as the external self is transformed; they serve as titles for the various editions of life. Thus in *Dom Casmurro*, Bentinho ("a little bit blessed") becomes Bento ("blessed") and then Santiago ("Saint Iago," in Helen Caldwell's interpretation); at the end of his life, he is Dom Casmurro, the old codger (Caldwell, 1960: 40–4, 128–9).

Music can provide another sort of text. It too can be used to fix a certain moment in time; the street vendors' cries in *Dom Casmurro* and in *Aires' Memorial* (*Memorial de Aires*) are examples of this process. But because musical texts are auditory rather than visual, they must be inherently ephemeral. Two of Machado's best stories, "Wedding Song" ("Cantiga de Esponsais") and "A Famous Man" ("Um Homem Célebre") deal directly with the difficulties of creating and utilizing musical texts to order and understand change (1962:II, 386–90, 497–504).

The written word – as it is inscribed on the page and as it is read – is more concrete than music, but it is no less ambiguous and ultimately unreliable. Perhaps the most fascinating aspect of Machado's novels for modern readers and critics is his obsession with the ways in which written texts are created and perceived. The narrators of his later works speculate and pontificate at length about the problems they face as authors and the problems they create for us as their readers.

Machado, in fact, used the creation of a written text – or, more precisely, of a set of written texts – as the most basic of his metaphors for the transformations of the external self as it moves through time and through society: Life is a series of editions. The metaphor is linear, in that each edition is a discrete unit, a document of one phase in the process of transformation; it is also cyclical, since each edition represents a return to the past, necessarily reformulating and emending those which preceded it. This idea seems strikingly original when Braz Cubas presents it, but it derives from one of the most commonplace images for change in Brazilian Romanticism, an image that Machado had used as the basis for the titles of his first two collections of verse: The *Chrysalids* (*Crisálidas*) of 1864 became the *Moths* (*Falenas*) of 1870.

The duality inherent in the written text strongly influences its form in Machado's major novels. The most extreme example of the formal parallel is Counselor Aires' *Memorial*, in which each diary entry maintains a chronologically based linear progression, while simultaneously referring to and reinterpreting previous entries. In *Dom Casmurro* and the *Posthumous Memoirs of Braz Cubas*, the same effect is achieved through the juxtaposition of a linear, autobiographical narrative and constant digressions that usually originate in the narrators' recollection of earlier texts, whether written, musical, human, or artifactual.

Thus the written text of the narrative, which purports to be one edition of the narrator's life and a document of considerable utility in ordering experience, is itself an anthology of previous editions or texts. We, as readers, must decide if these texts really belong in the anthology at all – determining that they are not entirely linear and random – and whether their order is rational and meaningful. It is their creators' purpose to convince themselves, and us, that they control reality, and that they can properly arrange it and understand it. The order they choose to present to us is often circular, symbolically denying change. Rubião, in *Quincas Borba*, goes back to Barbacena to die. Dom Casmurro arranges his various texts in an effort to "tie together the two points of life" (1962:I, 808). Braz Cubas, through the "extraordinary process" that he will not reveal to us, creates the posthumous narrative of his circular voyage "around life," linking his birth to his death (1962:I, 511, 510).

All of these narratives, whatever the apparent identities and motivations of their fictional creators, are of course Machado's own creations, editions of his own existence; Dom Casmurro's anthology of texts is but one text within Machado's superanthology, an evasive and ambiguous effort to document his own existence – not an autobiographical representation of his life, but a series of possible responses to the problems of identity and change that obsessed him.

Machado began writing fiction rather late in his literary career, but he was extraordinarily well prepared. Like Alencar, he had mastered the artificial, irreverent, and elitist style of the traditional *cronista* personality, very different from his own character. More important, he had created and perfected his own personal external identity – the erudite, aristocratic, and utterly refined man of letters – which allowed him to move along the racial continuum, and which was also his most astonishing fictive achievement.

In his first four novels, Machado sought to deal with the problems he was already beginning to define: the role of the external self and the conflict between the morality of the inner being, formed in the past, and the insistent demands of the future. The external self can attain future success and happiness only by obeying the dictates of ambition and accepting change. This conflict leads to irony, if not to tragedy, in all of Machado's early fiction.

Machado's unhappiness with the tradition of the standard Romantic novel of urban life, as he inherited it from Alencar, is also evident in these early works. These four novels can be seen, in part, as satires on that tradition and the comfortable vision of the world it presupposed (see Mac Adam, 1972). Machado's intrusive and often pompous third-person narrators claim to be omniscient, but they often mislead us and fail to bring the characters they describe to the happy endings Brazilian readers had come to expect.

The *Posthumous Memoirs of Braz Cubas* represented a considerable departure from these early novels, but the shift was evolutionary rather than revolutionary. Machado's major stylistic innovation was to replace the serious and at least superficially reliable narrator of his previous works with the openly unreliable and sardonic voice of the *cronista* personality, a voice he utilized again as the anonymous third-person narrator of *Quincas Borba*. Braz Cubas is outwardly very different from Machado de Assis: He is well-born, and birth and chance combine to insulate his external self from the harsher realities of the struggle for success that Machado had been forced to confront. This narrative is larger, in its chronological scope, than Machado's earlier works, and it contains a clear cyclical structure, imposed by Braz himself; such a framework had only been hinted at in *Resurrection* (*Ressurreição*) and *Yayá Garcia*. The problems Braz Cubas faces in the life he re-creates as a text are variations on issues Machado had raised earlier in less coherent and detailed form:

the nature of identity, the nature of time and change, the conflict between morality and ambition.

Braz's social and financial security largely free him from the most basic imperatives of the external soul as it moves through society, imperatives that can be seen more clearly in minor characters like Eugênia and Marcela. Braz, on the other hand, is far more preoccupied with the nature and effect of change as a function of time, and the one desire of his external self is to defeat time by accomplishing something of lasting importance. He fails utterly to achieve this goal during his lifetime; his only creation is his posthumous, savagely ironic re-creation of that failure.

Quincas Borba, the second of Machado's great novels, focuses more sharply on the demands of the external self, and upon the changes and imbalances that movement through society can create. Almost all of the characters are driven by the dictates of their external identities to ignore morality, thereby betraying themselves and others. Rubião's greatest tragedy is his absolute unawareness of the metamorphoses he undergoes during his voyage through time and society. His inability to find textual referents for those transformations makes him almost as oblivious as the dog who accompanies him on his circular journey. It is that lack of awareness which makes Rubião a mere pawn, manipulated by the Palhas and others, and exploited by the devious narrator, who suggests that Rubião's story proves the theory of Humanitism. Both morality and understanding, in fact, are almost entirely extratextual – in the mind and emotions of the reader, who is forced to the conclusion that society, the world of the external self, is viciously and inherently immoral, and that such immorality can be neither justified nor rationalized.

Dom Casmurro, the third of Machado's mature novels, is perhaps his best; it is also the most complex. For decades, Dom Casmurro's verdict about his wife was accepted without question: Capitu is an adulteress. Only recently have scholars, brilliantly led by Helen Caldwell, begun to make the case for her innocence (1960, 1970:142–9). In reality, however, the question of Capitu's guilt cannot be resolved one way or the other on the basis of Machado's text. I believe that this ambiguity is deliberate. The point of *Dom Casmurro* is that there is no single truth in the novelist's meticulous and subtle interweaving of two very different characters and their two very different stories.

The first story is that of Dom Casmurro himself, the creator of the text, whose two selves move through time rather than society. He is born wealthy and secure, without ambition; the only trace of his career as a lawyer is his text, which allows him to arrange the evidence and construct the most formidable case possible against Capitu. The circular structure of that text, moreover, denies time and change. This denial is reinforced by Dom Casmurro's explicit and implicit assertions that his internal self is still that of Bentinho Santiago at the age of sixteen – innocent and too trusting, easily manipulated by others because he is unaware of their ulterior motives and social ambitions. The narrator is unconscious, he makes clear, because his own external self has no ambition, and it is therefore easy for his ambitious wife, Capitu, to betray his trust with Escobar, his best friend. He has not changed, Dom Casmurro insists, but he is not so sure about Capitu. Wasn't she always inherently conscious – and therefore implicitly manipulative and potentially unfaithful? Or, he asks himself and us, did her original innocence turn to infidelity because he transformed her external self as he raised her to his own social level through marriage (1962:I, 942)?

Capitu's story is entirely different. She is indeed conscious, but only because she was born poor and dependent, without the luxury of Bento's conviction of unconsciousness. Her external identity is transformed by her marriage and the wealth it brings, but her internal self has not changed; she still thinks of herself as poor (1962:I, 909–10). This combination of external mobility and mutability and internal stability and regularity is symbolized by the sea that Bento sees when he looks into Capitu's eyes. The real ocean kills Escobar, but the tides Bento sees within Capitu are equally destructive, for their cyclical regularity reminds him of a fact he cannot and will not admit: It is his own internal self that has changed radically, even as his names have changed; Bento becomes Santiago, his own Iago, as he moves from innocence to insane suspicion.

Santiago represses his fantasy of infidelity with Sancha, Escobar's wife, sublimating his own guilt through his conviction of Capitu's unfaithfulness, and he wholly misinterprets the inherently ambiguous human text of their son to prove that infidelity. Dom Casmurro takes Capitu's abdication – her departure for Europe – as the final evidence of her guilt. Within the context of Capitu's parallel story, however, that decision results from her realization that the inner self of the Bentinho she first loved has been altered beyond recognition. She is resigned, as well, to the dependent, humiliated social position she had hoped to escape, a status symbolized by the song of the candy seller ("Cry, little girl; lament / For you don't have a cent") that remains, for Dom Casmurro, the most basic textual definition of their relationship (1962:I, 827, 913–14).

Although *Dom Casmurro* reflects Machado's general obsession with the effects of time and of both natural and social change, it also appears to be more autobiographical than his earlier works. There is some contemporary evidence that Machado was almost pathologically jealous of his white wife, Carolina (Basto Cordeiro, 1961:46); there are also ambiguous hints at mysterious events in her early life that might explain this jealousy (Massa, 1971:580–94). The novel's constant allusions to *Othello*, as Shakespeare's play and Verdi's opera, simultaneously reinforce Dom Casmurro's story of his wife's infidelity and Capitu's parallel tale of innocence betrayed by the jealousy of Santiago; those references to the noble Moor are, of course, particularly striking within the context of Machado's own marriage.

Other possible autobiographical references are hidden within onionskin layers of evasion. Helen Caldwell has argued quite convincingly that the anonymous author of one of Dom Casmurro's internal texts, the panegyric to Santa Monica, is essentially a portrait of Machado (1960:150–60). Thus Machado de Assis as author creates a text, the novel, in which a character named

Dom Casmurro creates a text that uses – and ridicules – a text created by a minor character who is really Machado himself.

Equally intriguing are the classical references embedded in another, artifactual text: the main room of Bento's childhood home, which he reconstructs in exact detail as part of his attempt to deny change, to link past and present. The four corners of the main room are painted to represent the four seasons, symbolizing natural, cyclical change. In the center of each of the four walls are medallions portraying four figures from Roman history: Julius Caesar, Augustus, Nero, and Masinissa. Each of these medallion texts serves a literary purpose within the novel, defining a series of possible relationships between men and their mothers and wives. Clarisse Bader's *La femme romaine* (1877), one of the major sources of Machado's classical references, can help us to understand the potential interpretations of those relationships.

Julius Caesar's wife was the perfect Roman matron, the ideal woman Bento sees in his mother, Dona Glória, and hopes to find in Capitu. Capitu, however, is much closer – at least according to Dom Casmurro – to Bader's vision of Augustus' wife, Livia Drusilla, a woman driven by ambition and therefore supremely conscious. "That wise wife, that loving mother did not see husband or child as other than the means to power." For Bader's Livia, as for Dom Casmurro's Capitu, "dissimulation was the true essence of her character, a dissimulation that was not natural to Augustus." Bader also reflected the general opinion that Livia poisoned Augustus (1877:115–35).

Nero, another suspected poisoner, ordered the death of his mother and killed his two wives. According to Bader, the second wife, Poppea, died when "Nero, in a fit of anger, killed the wife he loved with a blow from his foot. She was to be a mother; she died. The emperor" – and the parallel with Dom Casmurro and his text is inescapable – "gave her funeral oration. He could not bring her back to life; but he made her a goddess" (1877:183). The theme of poison, which appears in Machado's novel in the incident of the dogs Dom Casmurro tries to kill, as well as in

Dom Casmurro's inability to poison either himself or his son, is reinforced by the story of Masinissa. Machado's source here, in all probability, was Corneille's well-known tragedy. Masinissa was an enemy of Rome; when his wife Sophonisba was captured by the Romans, he sent her poison to eliminate her value as a hostage. She drank the poison and accepted her fate, as Capitu accepts the consequences of Santiago's jealousy.

Dom Casmurro's denunciation of Capitu is coupled with his extravagant, even blasphemous praise of his mother's fidelity and purity. In the text of her tombstone he declares that she was "A Saint," despite the contradictory hints about her real character that appear in her relationship with José Dias, Bento's surrogate father, and her possible interest in Escobar, her son's best friend (1962:I, 937–8). The anonymous, Machado-like author of the panegyric sings the praises of a genuine saint, Monica, who appears in the text created by her son, Saint Augustine, as the archetype of the loving and forgiving mother.

Some of these same references, however, form a separate internal text for Machado rather than for Dom Casmurro, a text with strong autobiographical implications. The figure of Julius Caesar may represent Machado's only reference to the epilepsy he shared with the first of the Julians. Other figures in this constellation of allusions refer to another hereditary defect, a *tara* about which Machado was even more reticent: his family's African origins. The three North Africans who appear as referents in Dom Casmurro's text – Othello, Masinissa, and Saint Augustine – all overcame their nonwhiteness (whether physical or merely geographical), and attained enormous social and political power. Nevertheless, both Othello and Masinissa failed to transform themselves totally, as Machado had done, and continued to define themselves as Africans rather than as Europeans; both were compelled to commit emotional suicide by killing the women they loved.

Saint Augustine is a happier case, and one more like Machado. Augustine not only transformed his personality, moving from rake to saint, but also successfully discarded the ideals and beliefs of his pagan past. Augustine, like Machado, left a text – his *Confessions*, one of Machado's favorite books – which documents his transformation through time and through society.[5] It is symptomatic of Machado's evasiveness, however, that he had already constructed a neatly ironic trap for those who might note this emphasis upon Saint Augustine and who might, therefore, theorize an autobiographical identification: The insanity of Quincas Borba, the mad philosopher of Humanitism, reaches its apex when he declares himself to be the reincarnation of Saint Augustine (1962:I, 649–50).

Machado's last two novels, *Esau and Jacob* (*Esaú e Jacó*) and *Aires' Memorial* (*Memorial de Aires*), have received relatively little critical attention. He clearly intended the two works to be read as a unit, and interwove their prefaces to make sure his readers understood this unity. Counselor Aires also appears as the author of both texts. Aires is a new sort of narrator for Machado, in both character and narrative technique. He is not bitter or ghost-ridden, but serene, almost Olympian – the sort of classical Greek statesman and savant that Joaquim Nabuco professed to see in Machado himself. The counselor is socially and financially secure, almost immune to the dictates of the external self; this self-confident retired diplomat appears, as well, to have buried both the sorrows and the pleasures of the past.

In *Esau and Jacob*, we have a third-person account of events in Rio de Janeiro over a fairly long period of time, from the prosperous 1860s, the high point of the Empire, to the Republic and the military dictatorship of the early 1890s. Aires, the author of this narrative, also appears as a minor character in it. This form sets Aires at some distance from us, as readers, and this distance is magnified by the nature of his discourse. Aires is not nearly so concerned with our response to his story as Braz Cubas, Dom Casmurro, or the narrator of *Quincas Borba*; he is reticent and ambiguous at times, but only because he is confused himself. If Aires sometimes misleads us – as in his search for referents for the two main characters in the story, Pedro and Paulo, who are variously linked to Esau and Jacob, Robespierre and Louis XVI,

Castor and Pollux, and the biblical Peter and Paul – it is because he is honestly unsure of the meaning of the characters and events he is describing.

The novel also represents a very considerable shift in Machado's focus on the problems of identity and change. In *Esau and Jacob*, the struggle of the external self to move upward through society is brilliantly portrayed in the careers of minor characters who are analogs of those we have met before, particularly in *Quincas Borba*: Santos, the money-mad banker, is a new version of Palha; Baptista, equally obsessed with politics, is very similar to Camacho; Nóbrega, the poor friar who becomes a millionaire, is a Rubião conscious of his fortune and in control of the new external identity it provides. All of these minor characters, moreover, are relatively happy, at peace with society and with themselves. The dictates of ambition have not created the destructive choices between morality and success found in earlier novels; their internal and external identities have, in general, retained a fundamental balance.

The problem of the individual's transformation by society is almost entirely restricted to the interplay of these supporting actors. The principal figures of *Esau and Jacob* – the lovely and tragic Flora and the twins she loves, Pedro and Paulo – are detailed and highly allegorical symbols of another problem, the nature of time as a catalyst for transformation. To set up his allegory, Machado again returned to his youth, to his Romantic verse and to his early fiction. At first glance, Pedro and Paulo appear to be a new version of the unstable, parasitic pairings of truncated identities found in a number of Machado's stories. Such relationships almost always end in betrayal, and some of Aires' referents – Esau and Jacob, for example – hint at the inevitability of similar treachery in the case of Pedro and Paulo. The twins certainly make every effort to do each other in, but they are too evenly matched for either to triumph; the conflict inherent in their relationship is therefore never resolved. No resolution is in fact possible, for Pedro and Paulo are not merely fictional characters, but allegorical representations of the past and the future.

Aires presents us with a text, offered as a possible explanation of the novel, from the fifth canto of Dante's *Inferno*: "*Dico, che quando l'anima mal nata...*" (1962:I, 945). Aires himself offers one interpretation of this text, which serves as his epigraph, applying the description "ignobly born souls" to Santos and his friends, a bunch of "insipid bores" who do not deserve the social and financial success they have attained (1962:I, 964). The Dante passage deals with the theme of predestination, as Minos assigns the souls who appear before him to the proper circle of Hell; *Esau and Jacob* contains frequent references to both moral and sociological predestination. The allusion to those badly or ignobly born may also reflect Machado's consistent preoccupation with beings, like himself or Braz Cubas' black butterfly, who were created with physical or social handicaps.

There is, however, another interpretation of Dante's phrase within the context of *Esau and Jacob*, an interpretation that I believe Machado's self-taught Italian facilitated.[6] The Italian adverb *mal* (or *male*) means "badly" or "ignobly"; in Portuguese, the cognate *mal* has the additional meanings of "barely," "scarcely." In this reading – far closer to the nineteenth-century social and biological determinism Machado had absorbed, however unwillingly – all beings are predestined by their birth and at the moment of birth: "I say that when the soul, barely born..." Pedro and Paulo are destined to fight from birth, symbolizing the conflict of past and future. This conflict is visible in Machado's early fiction – in *Resurrection, Helena,* and *Yayá Garcia,* for example – but here is raised to the level of a universal and eternal truth.

Within the artificial structure of *Esau and Jacob*, in fact, the past–future dialectic precedes birth, for the twins begin their fighting in Natividade's womb. We are told that Aires considered using the title *Ab ovo* (*From the Egg*) for his narrative (1962:I, 944); we know that Machado toyed with naming the twins' mother Conceição ("conception") rather than Natividade ("nativity").[7] The coexistence of past and future is symbolized, as well, by the moment Natividade chooses to tell her husband of her pregnancy: They are on their way home from a funeral, the inevitable human future.

Flora's name and nature refer directly back to Machado's early Romantic poetry. She is the momementary yet eternal present, torn between past and future – between Pedro and Paulo – and unable to reconcile the two; her death, like that of the heroine of Machado's early novel *Helena*, is the result of that inability. Flora is the Romantic flower, blooming for a brief instant before it must wither, the "Bud half-opened, rose half-closed, / Partly woman, partly child" of one of Machado's poems (1962:III, 209).

This allegory of chronological change is reinforced by Machado's utilization of social change – not the social transformation of the individual, here reserved for the minor characters, but the effects upon society as a whole of the passage of time. The story of Flora and the twins is set against the backdrop of fundamental political events: the abdication of Pedro II and the proclamation of the Republic in 1889. This historical moment is foreshadowed in the characters of Pedro and Paulo, who disagree about politics as about everything else except Flora: Pedro, as befits his name, is a monarchist; Paulo is a republican. The transformation of the Brazilian state, however, is as essentially meaningless as Pandora's other creations, and nothing really changes: Past and future remain separate and in conflict; Pedro becomes a Conservative, Paulo a Liberal.

Flora tries to use music as a text to define her existence, but musical texts, as we have seen, are too ephemeral. Aires survives the conflict between past and future because he accepts it, in his serene and austere old age, and because he is able to form events into a written text, thereby symbolically denying change. Custódio, the pastry chef, comes to Aires for advice in the construction of his own written text, the sign for his bakery. The counselor's advice is clear: Discard the past ("The Imperial Pastry Shop"); avoid commitment to a future ("The Pastry Shop of the Republic") that no one can ever predict, neither Bárbara the half-breed fortune teller nor Plácido the spiritualist, neither David nor the Sibyl; focus only upon the present existence of the self

("Custodio's Pastry Shop") (1962:I, 1026–8). Aires' narrative does not resolve the problem of time, therefore: It cannot be resolved. The old man merely uses his text to "kill time" (1962:I, 944), and we last see him fingering the flower in his buttonhole, the momentary present, like Flora, which forever blooms and withers (1962:I, 1091).

Machado appears to have planned *Esau and Jacob* as his last novel, his final word on the problems of time and change; its original title was *Último* (*The Last*). He went on, however, to write one last work, *Aires' Memorial*, which retains the counselor and his sister Rita. This new narrative has a different form – it is Aires' diary – but it is chronologically embedded in the earlier novel, dealing only with the period between 9 January 1888 and September of 1889. The *Memorial* has been almost ignored by critics, and most interpretations of the novel have been distorted by Machado's own hints that it contains autobiographical elements (1962:III, 1084, 1086). Two relatively minor figures in the *Memorial* – Aguiar and Dona Carmo, a Brazilian Darby and Joan – are said to be portraits of Machado and Carolina; Fidélia, the novel's heroine, has also been described as a younger version of Carolina, an identification buttressed by apparent confusion in the naming of characters in Machado's manuscript of the novel.

There are, however, serious problems with this autobiographical interpretation. First, the manuscript evidence is as unreliable as any other key to understanding Machado's life and works.[8] Secondly, his hints of autobiographical content are entirely out of character. Machado was intensely secretive about his private life and publicly insisted that his works had absolutely no connection with his life; as we have seen, the autobiographical references that do exist – in *Dom Casmurro*, for example – are extremely elusive and ambiguous. Finally, the character of Dona Carmo – sweet, gracious, voluble, and not too bright – does not greatly resemble the Carolina we encounter in photographs and in the recollections of those who knew her, a taciturn, undemonstrative matron whose favorite reading was a French translation of Dostoevski's *House of the Dead* (Basto Cordeiro, 1961:15, 62). Though

Machado may simply have been sentimentalizing the memory of his late wife, it is equally possible that Machado – the meticulous creator of the external self upon which his acceptance and success was based, the author of so many ambiguous texts by unreliable narrators – used the characters of Aguiar and Carmo, suitably highlighted by carefully chosen revelations to curious and loquacious friends, to extend the parameters of his created external self beyond the chronological limits of his own life.

The speculation Machado's hints encouraged, moreover, has often prevented critics from understanding *Aires' Memorial* as a novel, a fictive creation in which he once again focused upon the problem of chronological change. The dialectic of past and future that destroyed Flora in *Esau and Jacob* is altered in the *Memorial*. Fidélia has three choices rather than two: the past (her previous marriage and her devotion to her late husband's memory); the momentary present of old Aires himself, who toys with the idea – one that appears to mean more to him than his reticence will allow him to reveal openly[9] – of offering himself to the young widow; and the future with the young and handsome Tristão. Fidélia manages to overcome the past and love again. She never has to reject Aires, for he and Fidélia both realize that he is emotionally if not physically impotent. The line from Shelley, "I can give not what men call love," which Aires tries to present to himself and to us as a valid description of Fidélia, in fact sums up his own situation (1962:I, 1102–3).

Aires' account of Flora's life, as we have seen, restated the Romantic commonplace of the rosebud. The *Memorial* is a fictional version of yet another Romantic standard, the tearful farewell of the poet doomed to an early death. Aires is not young, and he is serene rather than lachrymose, but his diary is a long farewell to the past as he accepts the future, even the death implicit in that future. In the most basic of terms, the *Memorial* as a whole is about letting go – of the past, of love, of the problems of existence, of existence itself.

All of the characters in Aires' diary abdicate in one way or another. Fidélia leaves both past and present behind, and she and Tristão leave Brazil for Portugal and a new life in a future that belongs only to the young. Aguiar and Carmo are forced to confront their childlessness when their adopted children marry and depart; the only consolation the old couple finds is their love for each other – or, more precisely and ironically, their silent nostalgia for the love shared by the two beings they once were.

Aires himself has discarded the ambitions of the external self, which once ruled his existence. He has no children, and the wife he married to advance his career is buried in Europe and almost forgotten. His halfhearted fantasies about Fidélia are the last flickerings of his longing to love and be loved. All that remains, in the end, is his text, which Aires writes for himself rather than for us. Unlike Machado's earlier narrators and unlike the Aires of *Esau and Jacob*, the old man no longer cares about our response as his readers; he speaks only to the artifacts, the paper and pen, that he uses to create his text. He eventually abandons the diary itself: The final entry is undated, symbolizing his renunciation of even this attempt to control and order time.

Aires' farewell takes place within the context of historical events in Brazil. Whereas political change (the proclamation of the Republic) appears in *Esau and Jacob* as one of a number of referents for the past–future dialectic, Machado's use of history in the *Memorial* is far more subtle and sophisticated. A central event in Aires' diary is Abolition, the moment when Brazil let go of slavery. We can only guess at the profound meaning the "Golden Law" of 13 May 1888 held for Machado, the descendent of slaves; he carefully hid his reactions behind those of Aires. The old diplomat is pleased, on the whole, declaring that it was long since time to give up the "peculiar institution" that had so marred Brazil's international reputation (1962:I, 1116).

Other characters in the *Memorial* also confront the implications of Abolition. Fidélia's father, the Baron of Santa Pia, who is neither saintly nor pious, plans to free all his slaves; his motives are not humanitarian, however, but reflect his bitterness at the government's betrayal of his financial interests. When Fidélia inherits his estates and chattels, she goes even further than the "Golden Law" in discarding the institution of slavery and the patriarchal system built upon it. She divides her vast lands among the new freedmen, an act symbolizing the formation of both a new society and a new economy. She will not participate in the new world her generosity helps create, however: Her future lies with Tristão in Portugal.

Emancipation, moreover, is not the only historical event in Machado's allegory of renunciation and abdication. Machado's readers when the novel was published, in 1908, would have been intensely conscious of the implications of the dates in the *Memorial*; Aires abandons his diary almost exactly one month before the proclamation of the Republic. That proclamation, implicit in Aires' chronology, represents another new beginning for the nation, like Fidélia's gift to the freedmen. It is also, however, a very poignant renunciation of the past. The departure of Tristão and Fidélia for their future in Portugal forms one element in a symbolic trio. The second is the abdication and exile of an old man, Emperor Pedro II, who sailed away from Brazil, in November of 1889, to die in European exile. The third is Aires' own departure, as he puts aside his diary and thereby abdicates his existence in our consciousness.

Machado chose two epigraphs, drawn from medieval Portuguese poetry, for the *Memorial* (1962:I, 1093):

> There in Lisbon, by the sea,
> New ships I ordered built for me.
> A *cantiga* of Joham Zorro

> To see my lover fair,
> Who with me a tryst did swear,
>   I am away, mother.
> To see my lover now,
> Who with me a tryst did vow,
>   I am away, mother.
> King Dom Dinis

These quotations sum up the departures of Aires, of Fidélia and Tristão, and of Dom Pedro II. Fidélia's ability to love is reborn, and she sets sail on the new, Portuguese ship of her future, leaving her Brazilian past behind. Pedro II also leaves Brazil for Europe; his destination, ordained by political and social change, is not a new life, but death in exile. Pedro's abdication is employed, in a symbolic sense, to link the voyage of Tristão and Fidélia to Aires' renunciation of existence in a replication of a theme found in earlier writers: the return to the sea – and, implicitly, to the Portuguese past – as a metaphor for death. Aires gives up his diary in September of 1889; that decision presages the beginning of his own final journey, one imposed by the chronology of natural rather than social change. Aires' destination, however, is the same as that of Pedro II: the embrace of death, the beloved at last recognized and awaited.

The vessel on which Aires is about to set sail is not merely the ship of death, however; it also represents the decaying hulk of the Brazilian past, a ghostly derelict of lost ideals. Aires has buried his own past and will shortly cease his effort to create a text, but one part of the national past, one series of documentary texts, can never be left behind. As he muses about the meaning of Abolition, the old diplomat declares that although all the documents dealing with the African slave trade to Brazil may be burned – a step that the Republic in fact ordered two years after the passage of the "Golden Law," as Machado and his readers in 1908 knew very well – other texts will always remain: Heine's poem about a slaver bound for Rio de Janeiro, for example.

Aires, like Machado, pretends that Abolition has no personal meaning for him.[10] That claim is negated, however, by the text of the *Memorial.* A few lines after his description of Abolition and his allusion to Heine's "The Slave Ship," with its references to the sale of black slaves in Rio de Janeiro, Aires appears to move on to other, less momentous concerns. His sister is planning to let go of the artifactual texts of her life, her paintings, furniture, and books, and asks Aires to find her an auctioneer. Her request leads the counselor to contemplate the ultimate disposition of his own series of texts. He declares that the artifacts that define his external identity can all be liquidated privately, after his death – at a discount, if necessary. Aires' mental inventory of articles to be sold off, however, includes his original, natural identity – his own skin, which might well be utilized, he tells us, to construct "some primitive tom-tom or rustic drum" (1962:I, 1117).

Through Aires, Machado here is talking about himself. Despite all his social and literary success, despite his apotheosis as the first president of the Brazilian Academy of Letters, the *Memorial* strongly suggests that Machado continued to see himself, at some very basic level of his existence, as a captive aboard the slave ship of the national past and of his own ancestors. The poetic record of the enslavement and sale of his African forebears could not be erased, nor could he escape the fundamental textual evidence of his skin, which Aires' ironic musings link both to the Rio slave market and to the distant drums of Africa and of the plantation. Thanks to the efforts of Machado's biographers, we can trace his passage from Livramento Hill to the salons of the aristocracy; we can follow the transformations of his external identity as talent and ambition moved him upward through society. His internal identity, and the effects upon that identity of social change and of the destructive choices upon which such upward movement appeared to be based, can only occasionally be glimpsed in the dark mirror of the complex and ambiguous text Machado de Assis created to document his journey through the escape hatch.

6

The Black Swan:
João da Cruz e Sousa

In 1898, one year after Machado de Assis became president of
the Academy of Letters, an almost unknown young poet died in
poverty and obscurity. João da Cruz e Sousa, the leader of Brazilian Symbolism, was not one of Machado's "happy few" (Cândido,
1970:16). Many of the first academicians were Parnassian poets,
members of a movement that had established itself as a major

force in the nation's verse between 1885 and 1890. In their ideology, if not always in their poems, the Parnassians rejected the Romantic vision of the divinely inspired bard, a creative force exempt from the constraints of society and of form. They insisted that anyone willing to spend the time and effort could produce a perfect poem, defined by Parnassian theory as a metrically and grammatically correct and emotionally objective description of a landscape, a painting or sculpture, an oriental vase, or any of the imported *objets d'art* that were the beloved artifactual texts of the new rich of the early Republic. The leading poets of Parnassianism, like Machado, were utterly respectable and middle classs, good family men; many were bureaucrats, and they were proud that they had freed poets from "the obligation to wear their hair long" (Bilac, in Broca, 1960:7).

Symbolism was enormously influential in almost every other Western culture; it never had a chance in Brazil, in a literary world dominated by Parnassianism and its disciples. The nation's first Symbolists, who began publishing around 1890, were excluded from the Academy and other important cultural institutions. Parnassianism, *démodé* in Paris by 1880, managed to remain the dominant poetic movement in Brazil until the second decade of the twentieth century. One factor in Symbolism's failure to gain a foothold, moreover, was the Brazilian elite's inability to accept and understand the acknowledged leader of this new literary generation, João da Cruz e Sousa.

Cruz e Sousa, quite simply, shocked and baffled his contemporaries in Brazil, not only because the purpose and the form of his works were new and alien, but because he was black. As Sílvio Romero put it in 1899, Cruz e Sousa was at that point "the only case – in the whole development of Brazilian culture – of a black, a pure black, who was truly superior" (1960:V, 1686). He was not a mulatto, whose talent and intelligence could always be explained as the inevitable result of white genes. He was very dark, with entirely African somatic traits, and despite his culture and refinement, Cruz e Sousa could not be perceived as anything other than black. He was justifiably proud of his ability and accomplishments, but the white world was shocked and angered by his display of pride, which seemed aggressive and insolent. Cruz e Sousa, moreover, refused to make any gesture of compromise,[1] and scornfully described the literary world that rejected him as a collection of uniformly mediocre cretins, "darling little imbeciles gilded with facile popularity" (1961:451).

Cruz e Sousa baffled and disquited even those white writers who saw themselves as his friends and disciples, and their recollections often reveal a patronizing and grating prejudice. Their association with him, in fact, seems frequently to have been a form of self-seeking bohemianism, a way to get attention; the black poet recognized the superficiality of their friendship and their rebelliousness:

Many called themselves defiant rebels, but I knew the cheap tricks that were the basis for this rebellion, this defiance. Rebels only because they once went hungry for an hour, because they once walked in worn-out shoes. Defiant only out of spite that they had failed to grasp the futile little positions, which seemed to them so very glorious, that others had obtained...Rebellion and defiance only when safe at home; a kind of school-boy atheism – very zealous to cast down idols, but with prayers and amulets always close to hand in case it should thunder. [1961:654]

Even Nestor Vítor, Cruz e Sousa's closest friend, saw him less as a person than as a freak of nature, a mysterious and alien genetic accident: "The reincarnation of a Nubian from the days of David, or at least of Solomon,...Cruz e Sousa reveals himself, as an artist, as above all a sensualist – in the broadest meaning of the word; and this is simply logical in a primitive nature, most especially in an African" (Vítor, 1969:465).

Cruz e Sousa was born in what is now Florianópolis, the capital of Santa Catarina, in 1861. His father was a slave; his mother, freed shortly before his birth, was a laundress. His father's owners took an interest in the boy, and their support and his own obvious talents enabled him to receive the kind of education normally reserved for the province's elite. As a journalist and an aspiring poet, Cruz e Sousa quickly became an important figure in the low-key intellectual life of his native city, and the sons of some of Santa Catarina's most illustrious families were his friends. Prejudice and humiliation always lay just beneath the surface, however; those same friends used to make fun of his father as the half-simian "missing link" of Darwin (in Coutinho, 1979:62).

Cruz e Sousa settled in Rio de Janeiro in 1890 and eked out a living as a journalist. In 1893 he found a publisher for two of his books, *Missal* and *Shields* (*Broquéis*), and married Gavita Rosa Gonçalves, an educated black girl who worked as a seamstress (Magalhães Júnior, 1975:227–34). Cruz e Sousa had been very strongly influenced by Darwinism as a young man, and he appears to have been convinced that his marriage to Gavita represented a triumph of natural selection; they could produce, he believed, a new generation of intelligent and talented blacks who would be able to defy prejudice. Gavita bore a son for every year of their marriage.

Life was terribly difficult, however. Cruz e Sousa's two books were either ignored or violently criticized, and anonymous satires ridiculed both his style and his race:

Shield
(Sousa e Cruz)

A spiritualizing, half-wit dunce
Brought up in distant Mozambique
Has picked at true Art with his beak,
Swaying sickly, with sonorous grunts.
And all the blacks from Senegal
Do a buck-and-wing as they caterwall
And hail him with rockets bursting in air.
[in Magalhães Júnior, 1975:243]

The poet's refusal to hand out "compliments right and left, so as not to offend the vanity and presumption around him," and the hostility of the Parnassian establishment made a stable career in journalism very difficult. He was forced to take a job as a file clerk for the Central Railroad, and hated the work and his superiors there; above all, he was enraged that his "noble hands, made to harvest stars, have always to paw through the dirt, the feces, the debris of the human race" (1961:510).

The struggle was too much for Gavita, and she went insane in March of 1896; she spent much of the next six months in a cataleptic trance, sobbing fragments of childhood prayers. By the time she began to recover, her husband was dying of tuberculosis. His friends raised a little money by public subscription to send him to a spa in Minas Gerais in March of 1898; he died there, only four days after his arrival. The Central Railroad shipped Cruz e Sousa's body back to Rio de Janeiro, wrapped in old newspapers and lying on the filthy floor of an empty cattle car. New public appeals raised the equivalent of about ninety dollars to support Gavita and their four children; when she died of tuberculosis in 1901, two of her sons had already succumbed to the same disease, and the third followed within a few months. João da Cruz e Sousa Júnior, the poet's last and posthumous son, died of tuberculosis in 1915, at the age of seventeen.[2]

Critical reaction to Cruz e Sousa's works during his lifetime was almost uniformly hostile. José Veríssimo described *Missal* as "a heap of words which seem to have been chosen at random, like chances drawn from a hat, and placed one after the other in whatever order they come out" (1976:I, 80). This is the same critic, of course, who said he had serious doubts that "Mallarmé will ever achieve any kind of reputation as a French writer" (Góes, 1966:65), but Cruz e Sousa's repudiation by his contemporaries was due as much to his race as to differences in literary taste. Even those who tried hard to find something nice to say were painfully patronizing. Tristão de Alencar Araripe Júnior characterized Cruz e Sousa as primitive and ingenuous, the survivor of a race that had contributed brute strength rather than intelligence to the nation, an ignorant black urchin dazzled by the bright lights of the big city and by the trade beads of European culture (1963:147).

Cruz e Sousa was almost forgotten after his death, although Nestor Vítor faithfully organized the manuscripts the poet had left, publishing two volumes of poems – *Beacons* (*Faróis*) in 1900 and *Last Sonnets* (*Últimos Sonetos*) in 1905 – and the prose poems of the *Evocations* (*Evocações*), which appeared in 1898. *Shields* and *Missal* were not reedited until Vítor published Cruz e Sousa's complete works in 1923–4. Critical comments were both rare and condescending well into the third decade of this century; even today, some Brazilian critics have continued to stress Vítor's characterization of his friend as an atavistic throwback whose poetic style was wholly conditioned by his race. These descriptions of Cruz e Sousa's works as essentially African do not admit black intellectual and artistic contributions to Brazilian culture; they seek instead to avoid considering the poet within the context of Brazil – using his African genes to explain his verbal brilliance but refusing to recognize either his intelligence or his erudition. Agripino Grieco, for example, defined Cruz e Sousa as "the most instinctive, most spontaneous of poets," who had "read almost nothing," whose primitive and "sublimely ignorant" soul "divined or remembered . . . all things, but did not learn them in libraries" (n.d.:108).

The publication of Roger Bastide's study of Afro-Brazilian poetry (1943) transformed Cruz e Sousa's reputation. Brazilian intellectuals seem to have been stunned to discover that an illustrious French scholar considered Cruz e Sousa the equal of Mallarmé and Stefan George, and they reread the poet's works with a new respect. However, Bastide's orientation to some extent negated the value of his praise: He described Cruz e Sousa as a typical nonwhite Brazilian intellectual, like Tobias Barreto or Machado de Assis, who turned to literature in order to whiten himself socially, driven by an "immense longing to become an Aryan" and drawn to Symbolism because of its Northern European, Aryan origins (in Coutinho, 1979:157–63). Most critics since 1943 have accepted Bastide's thesis that Cruz e Sousa wanted only to be white, and have also continued to insist that he was merely an instinctive and unconscious poet, a primitive being enraptured by words and sounds (Pauli, n.d.:145–7).

I believe that these judgments are largely erroneous. Cruz e Sousa's conscious artistry and his universal importance have yet to be fully appreciated and recognized. I consider him the greatest of all nineteenth-century Brazilian poets, and far and away the greatest poet of African descent to appear in the Americas before the twentieth century. In my view, moreover, the fundamental purpose of much of Cruz e Sousa's poetry and prose was to affirm blackness rather than to reject it. The shock of Cruz e Sousa, for modern, non-Brazilian readers, is not his race; it is the fact that he was successfully attempting, at the end of the nineteenth century and within the stylistic confines of Symbolism, to confront ideological and formal problems that we tend to regard as uniquely twentieth-century, problems that are still being explored by African, Caribbean, and Afro-American writers.

The most basic of these problems was identity. Machado de Assis, moving inexorably toward the white end of the racial continuum to full social acceptance, defined the identity problem in universal, nonracial terms: the conflict between the internal and external selves. Cruz e Sousa, trapped by ancestry and somatology at the other extreme of the continuum, was both more open and more personal. He once may have hoped, in his youth, that he would be accepted for his talent alone, but those hopes must have quickly vanished. Unlike the somatically more acceptable Machado, Cruz e Sousa was forced to recognize and deal with his blackness; neither his culture nor his white friends could shield him from constant encounters with prejudice in cafes and barbershops (Jorge, 1957:130). Acceptance of his blackness and his African origins, however, was coupled with a realization that he was also simultaneously and irrevocably white – in his education and his culture. His prose self-portraits thus provide a universal paradigm of the dilemma of the black intellectual in our own time: how to find and express pride in self and race through the intellectual and linguistic structures of an alien culture, when the acquisition of that culture requires the assimilation of ideas and attitudes inherently destructive of that pride.

The Darwinism Cruz e Sousa absorbed as a young man in Santa Catarina postulated that some organisms within a species are clearly superior; he believed that he was such an organism, superior in intelligence and in sensibility, designed to produce literature. He immersed himself in white, European culture, mastering its ideas and its language. That culture, however, also insisted that those of African descent, Haeckel's woolly-haired *ulotrichi*, were "incapable of a true inner culture and of a higher mental development," and were clearly a species closer to gorillas than to men (Haeckel, 1876:II, 307–14, 363–6).

Thus, when Cruz e Sousa looked in the mirror, it was hard to avoid the self-hatred his whitened culture encouraged. "You come straight out of Darwin," he wrote of himself; "I can clearly see your overhung brow, the heritage of the orangutan; your lustful leer; the animalistic and rapacious air of the ape" (1961: 411). It seemed that only ever more learning and culture could negate the ape:

> I bore, like corpses lashed to my back and incessantly and interminably rotting, all the empiricisms of prejudice, the unknown layers of long-dead strata, of curious and desolate African races that Physiology had doomed forever to nullity with the mocking papal laughter of Haeckel!...
> The soul that roared and cried out within me demanded to be set free; to seal it over required the application of large treatises, huge folios, the whole library of great Alexandria, a Babel and a Babylon of scientific methods and Latin texts...
> My soul was badly bent towards Africa; I had to make it perfectly straight, to pull it over to the side of Order, to make my emotions rise and fall as neatly as a good thermometer!
> [1961:650–1]

Erudition and refinement had made the relatively light-skinned Machado acceptable to the white world, but they could not change Cruz e Sousa's situation. As he wrote Virgílio Várzea,

> All the doors and passage-ways along the road of life are closed to me, a poor Aryan artist – yes, Aryan, because I acquired, by systematic study, all the qualities of that great race. To what end? A sad black man, detested by those with culture, beaten down by society, always humiliated, cast out of every bed, spat upon in every household like some evil leper! But how? To be an artist with this color?
> [In Magalhães Júnior, 1975: 130–1]

Social rejection forced Cruz e Sousa back to his race, and back to the African heritage. Africa was very hard to find, however, at least at the intellectual level his whitened sophistication required. In the sources available to him, what knowledge of the continent existed was often vague and fragmentary; much of it dealt only with the area north of the Sahara – ancient Egypt and Babylon, nomad tribesmen, hot winds blowing across desert sand. What little Cruz e Sousa could learn of sub-Saharan Africa was distorted by the prejudices of white explorers, missionaries, and ethnologists.

Another Africa existed all around Cruz e Sousa – the cultural survivals of the African past preserved in the customs and celebrations of slaves and freedmen in Brazil. But the poet had lost contact with that world; he had isolated and alienated himself by the very culture he had absorbed in his futile attempt to move along the racial continuum, and he could no longer go back. In one of his *Evocations*, Cruz e Sousa describes an encounter with a small group of masked dancers – black figures leaping to the sound of drums – during Carnival. He first perceives the dancers through the whitened eyes of European culture, and is offended and repelled, "as if slugs were feeding on my body,...slugs leaving their tracks of slime in my mouth." With this nausea, however, comes pain, a complex ironic pain that he cannot join the dancers, cannot regain what education has erased, cannot fully identify himself with them and with "this race of night, shrouded in black night, from which I came through the mysteries of the cell, brought from far away and cast into life by the creative mindlessness of the egg" (1961:538–9).

This primal pain became the basis for Cruz e Sousa's identity. In racial terms, he defined the African past as a tapestry of pain – the misery of deserts, of slavery, of prejudice. On a more personal level, he was as much a slave as Africa itself, walled in forever by concentric barriers he could not surmount: His black vitality and intelligence had been encircled and suppressed by white erudition and aesthetics; his whitened intellect was trapped within a black body; that black body was surrounded by an alien and hostile white world (1961:663–4). The only solution was to accept blackness and its infinite and eternal pain. Indeed, the greatest glory of Africa and of her children, for Cruz e Sousa, was the ability to endure this pain and survive: .

Black Pain

Blood-spattered and black, formed of lava and of darkness, of torment and of tears, . . . what kind of life is this, which even stones reject, which even the stars themselves have vainly bewailed for centuries?!

.   .   .

   There, singing an endless Requiem, sobbing and wailing, shrieking and gasping comic and deadly laughter within your blood, within the dark chalice of the Calvaries of your body – there is human Misery itself, chaining you to fetters, searing your belly with white-hot irons, crushing you with the hard and selfish jackboot of Civilization: all this in the false name of a tattered and ridiculous liberty; searing your mouth with a white-hot iron, searing your eyes with a white-hot iron, gruesomely dancing and leaping upon the clayey mud of the graveyards of your Dream.

   Thrice buried, thrice interred: in race, in savagery, in deserts; devoured by the solar conflagration as if by some burning leprosy of the skies. You are the black soul of dying moans, the black Nirvana, the wide and gloomy river of every hopeless sigh, the gigantic and night-black phantom of Desolation, the monstrous mountain of screams, mummification of all mummies, the crystallization of sphinxes, chained down by Race and by the World to suffer, without pity, the agony of superhuman Pain. Pain venomous and vast enough to blot out the sun as it couples in convulsive spasms with the moon – the dread rutting of the eclipse of Death – when the strange and colossal steeds of Destruction and Devastation gallop, gallop through Infinity, colossal, colossal, colossal…

[1961:525–6]

   The problem of Cruz e Sousa's audience was as critical, and as modern, as the question of identity. As Eglê Malheiros Miguel noted, those who could have understood Cruz e Sousa – other black Brazilians – were almost uniformly illiterate; those who could read, Brazil's whites, were unwilling or unable to comprehend his reactions to race and prejudice (in *Centenário*, 1962:44). The poet, therefore, was often writing for himself, as a kind of psychotherapy, to escape from the utter isolation of his life. He also wrote, he suggested, for readers who did not yet exist, for a new generation of educated blacks, symbolized by the children he and Gavita were producing, who would fully share his abilities and emotions. Nonetheless, Cruz e Sousa also felt that it was his destiny and his responsibility to try to reach his white contemporaries – particularly in *Missal* and *Shields*, published while he still hoped for acceptance and success.

Although Cruz e Sousa believed that art had to be intensely personal – that "its chief value consists in the personal character of its author," in the words of Eugène Véron, a French aesthetician who was one of his sources – he nevertheless appears to have also accepted Véron's insistence that

if a poet. . .be stirred by ideas or facts of a strangeness so novel as to be unintelligible to his contemporaries. . .he will live unnoticed and die in obscurity. The only way in which he can exercise his due influence upon his generation, is by reflecting some of the ideas, habits of thought, sentiments and aspirations which animate it.
[1879:104, 333]

I believe that the problem of audience was the decisive factor in Cruz e Sousa's decisions about style and form. He wanted (as Mallarmé said of Poe) to "give a new and purer meaning to the words of the tribe," but Cruz e Sousa faced a dilemma alien to both Mallarmé and Poe. The language in which Cruz e Sousa wrote – his only language, his only means to communicate his ideas and emotions – was not that of his tribe; he was forced to use a white, European tongue, in which explicit and implicit prejudice against his own race and color were deeply embedded. Cruz e Sousa, however, was determined to express pride as well as anguish, to describe the beauty of Gavita and their children in a language designed to sing the praises of fair white maidens and the "children of gold and rose" (1961:357). And he was determined, finally, to create a "new and remarkable visual interpretation of the color black" (1961:514).

His earliest poems, written while he was still in Santa Catarina, were Romantic in style, in large measure the product of his great admiration for Castro Alves as an abolitionist. Cruz e Sousa and his friends in the province later came to admire the "New Ones" ("Os Novos"), as the Parnassians were first described, and he began to attack the Romantic literary elite of Santa Catarina with a violence that reflected his growing social and racial bitterness. One traditional view is that Cruz e Sousa became a Symbolist only after his arrival in Rio de Janeiro, as a reaction against the Parnassian establishment there. Roger Bastide suggested, on the other hand, that Cruz e Sousa was attracted to Symbolism because he was fascinated by its whiteness, its Aryanness.

Both these explanations seem far too simplistic. Literary politics did play a role in Cruz e Sousa's stylistic development, but it is also a fact that many of the ideological and linguistic elements typical of his mature works can be found in essays be published in Santa Catarina as early as 1885 (1961:746–8). He certainly did wish, at times, that he were physically as well as intellectually white and European, but there were other, more basic reasons for his interest in Symbolism. He did not become a Symbolist simply because he longed to immerse himself in a world of snow, castles, and white princesses, but because he saw the potential utility of Symbolist ideas and techniques as he formulated his intensely personal style. Cruz e Sousa was not as erudite as Machado, but he was certainly not the ignorant primitive critics have so often portrayed; he had carefully read, in French, a number of important foreign authors: Hugo, Poe, Baudelaire, Rimbaud, Huysmans, Villiers de l'Isle Adam, Verlaine, Schopenhauer, perhaps Mallarmé and Jean Moréas. He borrowed consciously and selectively from his foreign sources as well as from his Brazilian predecessors.

Cruz e Sousa was first attracted, perhaps, by the Symbolist ideal – itself a throwback to Romanticism – of the poet as a singular being, different from other mortals and therefore destined to suffer. His friends in Rio de Janeiro attempted to set themselves apart through their bohemianism; as I have suggested, they used their association with the poet they called "The Black Swan" or "The Black Dante" as one element in their pose as decadents.[3] Cruz e Sousa had no need to pose: He was automatically perceived as different, by friends and enemies alike; his misery was real rather than feigned. The personal, even hermetic, nature of many of the foreign works he read also must have appealed to him as he struggled to balance his desire for self-expression with the limitations of his audience. Above all, Symbolism's ideas and techniques appeared to him to make it possible to create an artificial new poetic language, one that would allow him to overcome the limitations of white Portuguese and to communicate emotions alien to his white readers.

Cruz e Sousa was encouraged by his foreign models to expand the linguistic repertoire of Portuguese, creating entirely new words and reviving obsolete forms. Baudelaire's reputation as an obscene poet gave his Brazilian disciple passive permission to expand the poetic language in other directions, allowing Cruz e Sousa to ignore traditional moral constraints and push to the limits of scatology and gynecology – as in his account of the birth of one of his children, or the detailed description of the primordial sexuality of the "Dark Lady" ("Tenebrosa"): "your velvet vulva, . . . somber sanctuary of transfiguration, magic lantern of metamorphosis, primordial crucible of genital impurity, dusky fountain of ecstasy, of sad and spasmodic sighs, and of the orgasmic Torment of all life" (1961:518).

Another Symbolist technique adopted was synesthesia. Cruz e Sousa felt continually immersed in sensations; his extreme sensitivity to those sensations was both implicit in his function as poet and inherent in his African roots, he suggested. He reformulated somatic prejudice to explain this heightened sensivity, to turn liabilities into assets. Sounds had colors, as Rimbaud and others had claimed, and Cruz e Sousa began to associate vowels with whiteness, velar and labiodental fricatives with blackness. Sounds also possessed aromas, which only his broad African nose could capture and perceive (1961:486–7). His African lips could taste sounds as well; /v/, for example, had the taste of ripe, bittersweet fruit (1961:567–8).

These synesthetic correspondences, when combined with and reinforced by onomatopoeia and alliteration, could create powerful cumulative effects, as in Cruz e Sousa's almost untranslatable "Weeping of Guitars" ("Violões que Choram") (1961:124):

> Vozes veladas, veludosas vozes
> volúpias dos violões, vozes veladas
> vagam nos velhos vórtices velozes
> dos ventos, vivas, vãs, vulcanizadas.

(Veiled voices, velvet voices, the voluptuousness of guitars, veiled voices wander in the ancient, swift-moving vortices of the wind – alive, volcanic, vain.)

The throbbing /v/'s reproduce the sounds of the guitars (*violões*), which set up a series of sound-based associations focused upon those who play these instruments, dark-skinned beggars who are at once the fruits of nature and the eternal detritus of society.

In general, however, synethesia – for Cruz e Sousa as for Rimbaud – was perhaps more attractive in theory than in practice. The theory of the symbol itself was more immediately useful to Cruz e Sousa, as were the Neoplatonic abstractions that were the basis for both the *correspondences* of Baudelaire and Symbolist aesthetics. As Cruz e Sousa understood it, poetry's final purpose was not to describe, but to establish direct, nonverbal – or, more exactly, paraverbal – contact between the emotions of an author and those of his readers. Words had no poetic value when used within the context of daily existence; at this level, the word "sunset," for example, referred only to a particular sunset once witnessed, a single, personal experience devoid of any greater meaning. When raised to the level of symbol, however, "sunset" contained a series of experiences and associations all linked, in the poet's mind, to the *idea* of sunset rather than to an isolated astronomical event, and this ideal sunset could call forth harmonic emotions and associations in the minds of readers.

Cruz e Sousa often used capitalization to make the distinction between words-as-words and words-as-symbols. Thus *dor* was simple, physiological pain, one element in the linguistic code; *Dor* formed part of the symbolic code, representing the common pain of all humanity as it contemplates the inherent imperfection of existence. The symbolic code itself, however, was often binomial in Cruz e Sousa's works, composed of two separate and sometimes contradictory codes, perhaps best defined as the code of whiteness and the code of blackness. Thus *Dor* is both the generalized pain of human existence (the white code) and the separate existential pain of the African heritage, of blackness in a white world. For white readers, "Sunset" was an easily accessible, entirely traditional symbol; its associations and resonances in the white symbolic code included sadness, the cyclical inevitability of change and of death, fear of darkness, and so on. Within Cruz e Sousa's black symbolic code, however, "Sunset" represented the joyful triumph of darkness over light and the possibility of reintegration and renewal within the harmonic blackness of the night.

A clearer idea of Cruz e Sousa's Symbolism can be gained through analysis of *Shields* (*Broquéis*), his first volume of poetry in this style and the only one whose arrangement and editing he controlled fully. The volume's title refers to its central image of conflict; the timelessness of that conflict is implicit in the word *broquéis* – the round bucklers of medieval warfare. The roundness of these shields is replicated in the arrangement of texts within the book: Several longer poems present the ambiguous ideal of physical and moral purity (in the white symbolic code) and of whiteness (the black symbolic code); the sonnet sequences that fall between these longer poems explore the consequences of that double ideal, spiraling down to the level of human impurity before rising again to the sphere of perfection. This formal circularity is reinforced by a series of images of roundness: the Sun and Moon, the censers of Catholic altars, crystal goblets of wine and of poison, the breasts of women, the coiled tresses of lovers and the snake's coils, the pirouettes of the clown, the spirals of the whirlwind and of Hell.

The nature of the conflict in which these poems-shields are employed is set forth in "Antiphony" ("Antifonia"), which introduces the book and which also contains many of the symbolic elements utilized in the rest of the poems. The title of this introduction and its initial images make it clear that the conflict will be presented, at least on one level, within the symbolic context of Catholic beliefs and artifacts. After the first stanza, the second half of each quatrain begins, slowly and faintly at first, to introduce the antiphonal voice, to suggest that there are problems inherent in an obsession with whiteness and purity, and to imply alternatives.

> Oh white, alabastrine Forms, bright Forms
> of moonlight, snow, and mists!...
> Oh cloudy, fluid, crystalline Forms...
> Frankincense burning on altars high...
>
> Forms, pure as starlight, of the Love
> of misty Virgins and Saints...
> Will-o'-the-wisps, things dewy fresh,
> the sorrows of the lily and the rose...
>
> Half-heard strains, celestial music,
> harmonies of Color and Perfume...
> Sunset hours, tremulously final,
> Requiem distilling the Pain of Light...
>
> Visions, psalms, and canticles serene,
> pianissimos of sickly, sobbing organs...
> The lethargy of lust-filled poisons,
> soft and subtle, deadly yet bright...

In the fifth stanza, the poet breaks into the antiphony to invoke the "infinite, edenic, airy" spirits of Art, and begs them to make his imagination fertile; he then goes on, in the next stanzas, to ask that the "golden pollen of the highest stars" fertilize the poetic forms that imagination will find to represent the ideal, Neoplatonic Forms. The eighth stanza returns to the female figures of the second four lines of the poem, but these figures are now carnal rather than spiritual; the next eight lines suggest the deep longings of the flesh and the harshness of the conflict between spirituality and carnality:

> Crystals diluted by the sudden gleam
> of anguish, tumults, courage, and desire;
> tawny victories and bitter triumphs,
> the strangest of all tremblings...

> Black blooms of boredom and vague blooms
> of vain, tantalic, sickly loves...
> Scarlet depths of ancient wounds
> open in blood to river forth...

"Antiphony" ends with a final invocation:

> Let all come forth! nervous, alive
> and hot and strong, to pass in song,
> in the Dream's vain whirlwind, the dread face
> and cabalistic hordes of Death...[4]

The conflict of existence, as Cruz e Sousa sets it out in "Antiphony" and in the poems that follow it, is not merely between life and death, but also between acceptance of an imperfect reality and denial of life in order to pursue an inhuman, unattainable purity; it is a conflict, as well, between light and darkness, between whiteness and blackness. Two abstractions are fundamental elements in the creation of the philosophical and personal contexts of that conflict. The symbolic Dream, in these poems, is at once the common human longing for perfection, acceptance, and fulfillment (the white code) and Cruz e Sousa's personal Dream – inherent in his education and his situation – of physical as well as intellectual whiteness, and of the artistic and social success that whiteness would bring (the black code). Neither goal can be attained. Perfection demands a denial of the realities of the human condition, in the white symbolic code. Within the black code, the White Dream requires a self-destructive rejection of the poet's own blackness. Pain, the existential Pain of all mankind and Cruz e Sousa's own racial Pain, is the inevitable result of the frustration of both these Dreams.

The symbolic conflict between life and the Dream takes place at four levels: celestial, Catholic, carnal, and infernal. At the highest, the Sun symbolizes the force and fire of life, in the white code, and Cruz e Sousa's own heritage of the burning deserts and tropical forests of Africa. Alternating regularly and cyclically with the red fire of the Sun is an equally positive symbol – the serene, healing darkness of the night, equally alive and fertile. The alien intruder in this cosmology and the symbol of the destructive attraction of the Dream is the full Moon: pure yet dead, producing sterile light without heat, the source of madness.

At the level of Catholicism and its symbols and artifacts, the reality and vitality of life are found in popular celebrations of the fruitfulness of the Sun and Earth and man – the harvest festivals of wheat fields and vineyards – and in an iconography that reflects and accepts the imperfection of human existence through crucifixes of wood and clay and stone and dark bronze. This religion of the life-force is perverted and destroyed by the symbols of a rigid Catholicism indistinguishable from the White Dream: Christs of ivory and silver; white candles and clouds of incense; the Virgin, linked to the sterile full Moon as the Queen of Heaven; the saints and nuns who have denied their natural fertility and humanity in pursuit of a morbid chastity.

Various carnal relationships are suggested and described at the third level. Mankind, in the white code, longs for true Love, at once physical and mystical, the procreative basis of the future. Cruz e Sousa's personal carnal ideal, in the black code within these poems written before his marriage to Gavita, is the beloved who is his moral and physical equal and through whose fertility his existence can be continued. These longings, once again, are perverted by the Dream, which insists that the consummation of sexual love, "the strangest of all tremblings," is sinful and impure (the white code); the poet, in the black code, finds only sterile white virgins, adored from a distance as the physical manifestations of the frigid and sickly Dream, or equally sterile and loveless sexual encounters with black and white temptresses – the "black blooms of boredom" and, above all, the "vague blooms of vain, tantalic, sickly loves" of his "tawny victories," the conquest of white women like Lésbia in the poem of that name:

> Savage mandrake, lustful nightbane,
> deadly plant that feeds on flesh;
> from your bacchantic body rain
> scarlet explosions of living blood.

On your caustic, convulsive lips
Love – morose and tragic – laughs
and laughs with violent laughter; death
in frozen spasms slithers past...

Hysteric Lésbia, sickly, cruel,
idol, demon, serpent, fuel
for all the tempting flames of lust;

from the bitter, acidulous husks
of your breasts flow stupors, miasmas of musk –·
the opiates of a tubercular moon...[5]

The symbolism used to describe these carnal encounters is drawn from Catholicism as well, from the story of man's original Fall. The hair of the white temptress becomes a snake: the Serpent, the "Origin of Evil" (1961:91).[6] Her seduction of the poet repeats the tragedy of Eden; to neutralize the power of her body – itself the Edenic serpent, the "strange colossal worm," the "vile reptile in the mud" (1961:85) – the poet must equal her evil and her violence, transforming himself into the avenging black serpent of the phallus:

Lust

I would be the poisonous snake
that gives you nightmares, brings you fear,
to coil within – my lovely Flower –
the tawny whirlwinds of your hair.

I would be the velvet snake,
writhing in infinite coils beneath
to strike your soft and perfumed breasts
and slobbering tear them with my teeth...

Perhaps your flaming, polluted blood,
your languid and bacchantic flesh,
as drowsy as the Rhine's soft flood,

might strangely be made pure at last...
For only an equal venom kills
the hungry poison of the asp...[7]

Nestor Vítor noted, in typically patronizing fashion, that Cruz e Sousa had loved several white women before he met Gavita, "affairs that would have made any man of his color proud" (in Coutinho, 1979:131). Within the context of the poems, however, these sexual relationships, like religion and the contemplation of the heavens, are no more than one sort of shield, to be used in the struggle against the Dream and its Pain. Yet another shield – drawn from Catholicism, from his readings in Baudelaire and other writers, and from his own symbology of carnal love – is Cruz e Sousa's admiration for "caprine and rebellious" Satan, at the infernal level of the text (1961:80). Transformed by the white serpents of carnality into the black serpent of violence and revenge, the poet identifies with the original Tempter. That identification is intensified by the image of Satan as caprine, a word Cruz e Sousa also used to describe himself in his prose poems (1961: 484–92). The vocabulary of racial prejudice in Brazilian Portuguese defines black men as goatish, as *bodes* or *cabras*.[8] Cruz e Sousa took this highly pejorative characterization – based upon white belief in the animalistic nature, rank body odor, and indiscriminate sexual appetites of those of African descent – and applied it both to himself and to the horned, cloven-hoofed ruler of Hell.

That identification, however, is ultimately as useless and destructive a shield as the other defenses against Pain that Cruz e Sousa presents in this volume. If Catholicism perverts the life-force by wrapping it in the white shroud of a frigid, unattainable purity, Satanism negates the spirituality and the potential fertility of love, transforming it into the sterile lust of eunuchs or the last orgasmic twitch of a drooling, senile god of evil (1961:81, 95). Baudelaire had written that laughter "is one of the clearest traces of Satanism existing in man," a characteristic "closely connected with the calamity brought about by an ancient fall" (1923:376, 373). Satanic, cynical laughter rejects and perverts true emotion as surely as the crystalline canticles of ivory crucifixes or the sterility of the Virgin–Moon. For Cruz e Sousa, laughter is a shield, the evasive refuge of a black man in a white world; he may laugh – in Langston Hughes' phrase – to keep from crying as he contemplates the Dream and its Pain, but that laughter also makes the poet a self-destructive and ridiculous clown:

> Acrobat of Pain
> Laugh! Hah! Guffaw your aching laugh!
> A clown, a puppet hanging on a string.
> Laugh! nervous; laugh! absurd, bursting
> with violent irony and pain.
>
> Laugh! The bloody, harsh guffaw
> makes your bells tinkle; in convulsions
> leap! puppet; leap! my clown, torn
> by the rattle of lingering death...
>
> Encore! they cry; they will not be denied!
> Come on! Retense your muscles tight
> in these macabre pirouettes of steel...
>
> And though you fall choking to the ground
> to drown in your boiling, burning blood,
> laugh! my heart, the saddest clown.[9]

Cruz e Sousa's next volume of verse, *Beacons*, and his prose *Evocations* continued and intensified these themes and symbols, moving him closer to a full acceptance of blackness and of its Pain. The White Dream could be ignored, at least for a while, as he contemplated the beauty of Gavita, his "Nubian" (1961:422–4),[10] and of their children, or as he immersed himself in images of night, the "sweet and starry abyss, sleep-walking Nirvana,...where I may drink the elixir of forgetfulness and sleep" (1961:492). The Dream is always present, however, just below the surface of existence, as the envy of whiteness that Cruz e Sousa saw as the eternal weakness of Africa and her children, and that he personified – in an allusion strikingly similar to those of Machado de Assis – as the "accursed ghost of Iago" (1961:136–7).

There is, however, a new and more explicit rebelliousness in *Beacons*, as the poet identifies with all those who are "Beacons blown out at night / by howling, desperate winds" (1961:148). The title of the volume was taken from the sixth poem in Baudelaire's *Flowers of Evil*, "Les phares." Baudelaire wrote of the talents of great artists; Cruz e Sousa's beacons are not the famous, but the forgotten, "the miserable, the broken, / the flowers of sewer slime" (1961:147); not the brilliant, but those who absorb light or who stand out by their lack of light; all the "harsh cast-offs of man's misery and wrath" (1961:127); those trapped in the blackness of poverty; the blind, whose dead eyes are windows opened on interior blackness (1961:171–4); the insane, filled with another sort of darkness and lost in the shadows of "the distant mansions, / there where madness dwells" (1961:137); the drunkards of street corners, who scorn the golden wine of European sacraments and feasts to drown their Pain in the black wine of suffering and sin (1961:105–6, 171–4).

There is, as well, a new and more intense identification with the greatest of all the beacons of darkness: Lucifer, the lightbearer, "the sweet and archangelic Black God, the Trismegistus, with horns of bitter courage, with flashing, fluted, enigmatic wings, calmly contemplating the unthinkable Crime" (1961:648). That symbolic Crime – rebellion against God in the white code – was for Cruz e Sousa the one supreme and unforgivable sin, to be black and vital amid the "senile boredom of the shuttered heaven" (1961:650, 151) of a white and unfeeling Christian God, who had offered up his own son in a cruel and meaningless sacrifice:

> Good Friday
> A green, bewitching, absinthe moon,
> as witless as some monstrous vice...
> A strange dog scrabbles in the dung,
> howling at legendary skies.
>
> This is Good Friday – holy, dark!
> Christ is dead: a leper, vile
> and cold and wounded, eyes grown hard
> with Death, his blood now purple bile.
>
> The serpent of evil and of sin
> spreads its venom – dark, sea-green –
> across his Death, silent, serene.

The sacrifice. But from the Nazarene
blooms not some pure and holy Love,
but the phosphorescence of gangrene![11]

Cruz e Sousa's final book of poems, *Last Sonnets*, is quite different from these earlier works. Its poems, formed by Cruz e Sousa's despair at poverty, public failure, Gavita's insanity, and his own tuberculosis, were also strongly influenced by his readings in Schopenhauer (see Malinoff, 1976). With more than a trace of the "suicidal longings" he had described as characteristic of the African heritage and its envy of whiteness (1961:663), Cruz e Sousa sang of resignation rather than rebellion, accepting the German philosopher's ideal of pain as the force through which human existence is ultimately purified, so that it may be absorbed after death into the transcendental "Black Nirvana" of the afterlife. Death, the conquest of the "carnal abysses of the sad clay" of the flesh (1961:208), is the final liberation from the social and emotional consequences of blackness; the poet's soul will rise beyond both the vitality of the African Sun and the sterile destructiveness of the white Moon to become a star, filled with the light of true intelligence and talent, immersed in and reintegrated into the healing blackness of the night sky (1961:216–17), free at last of "the unknown Dream, / the serpent that maddens and tears" (1961:213).

These sonnets of resignation document the final victory of white Brazil. But despite all of Cruz e Sousa's zeal to be at last "free of enslaving matter, / to tear off the shackles that torture us" (1961:185) in order to achieve what Schopenhauer described as the "unshakable peace, a deep calm and inward serenity" of the denial of the will to live (1958:I, 389–90), Cruz e Sousa could not give up the last and strongest of his shields – his undying hatred of the world of whiteness he was soon to leave behind:

> Sacred Hate
> My hatred, my majestic loathing,
> hatred holy, healthy, pure –
> annoint my forehead with your kiss
> to make me humble yet secure.

Humble but generous to the meek;
haughty toward those without Desire
or Faith or Goodness or the gleam
of sunlight's rich and gentle fire.

My hatred is the blessed flag
that flies in my soul's infinity
while other holy banners drag;

the foes of Love corruption wield
from the seven towers of deadly Sin –
sweet, healthy hatred, be my shield![12]

7

From despair to Modernism

The period between about 1890 and 1930 was perhaps the most difficult of all for educated Brazilians interested in their nation and its future. During the years that immediately preceded this period, many of the elite had come to believe that almost everything wrong with Brazil could be blamed on two obsolete institutions: the monarchy and slavery. When neither Abolition nor the proclamation of the Republic brought about the profound changes Brazilians had come to expect, the inevitable result was a widespread sense of betrayal and disillusionment.[1]

A new explanation for national underdevelopment was therefore necessary. The traditional disquiet about the human element within the glorious national landscape was both reinforced and made respectable by the popularization of deterministic and ultimately racist theories of society. These theories, imported from Europe and North America, greatly strengthened the elite's belief in the inherent inferiority of the nation's population as a whole. All of modern science, at least in Brazilian eyes, appeared to point to a single conclusion: Nonwhites, whether of Indian or African descent, were clearly and irrevocably inferior, and the Portuguese and their descendants, as Mediterranean peoples, were themselves inferior to the inhabitants of northern, Aryan Europe (Romero and Ribeiro, 1909:xxxv–xxxvii).

The implications of these theories of the physical and intellectual inferiority of nonwhites were dispiriting, even frightening. The national census of 1890 showed that only 44 percent of Brazil's population was white; even that high a percentage is suspect, since the use of cultural and behavioral criteria to determine racial identity undoubtedly led census takers to count at least some nonwhites as genetically European (Skidmore, 1974:44–5, 67). It was extremely difficult, in the face of this census data, to envision the survival and modernization of a society so profoundly and extensively contaminated by the presence of inferior racial groups. It was widely believed, moreover, that those of mixed blood would be physically, intellectually, and morally degenerate – perhaps even inferior to pure-blooded Africans and Indians.

Brazilian Naturalism offers concrete evidence of the elite's disquiet about the nonwhite population. Naturalist novels were very popular in the decades immediately before and after Abolition, and although the theory of Naturalism – as interpreted in Brazil – drew heavily upon such foreign models as Zola, in practice the movement represented a fusion of European biological and social determinism with the stereotypes of the national abolitionist tradition. Almost all of the characters in the major novels of Brazilian Naturalism can be seen as victims of the past – a past that very frequently revolves around the institution of slavery – and of the predetermined defects or *taras* that perpetuate the past in the present. Nonwhites, whether slave or free, retain both the biological *taras* of racial inferiority and the social *taras* engendered in an environment marked by subservience, poverty, and hunger. White characters are no more capable of escape from the consequences of slavery. Thus Amâncio, the aristocratic young hero of Aluísio Azevedo's 1884 *Boarding House* (*Casa de Pensão*), is doomed from the start – brutalized by his slave-owning father, spoiled by his mother, and infected by the syphilitic milk of his black wet nurse (1965:19–24).

The theme of the best and most profound of the novels of Brazilian Naturalism, Adolfo Caminha's 1895 *Good Nigger* (*Bom-Crioulo*) is shocking even today – homosexuality in the Brazilian navy. Caminha (1867–97) was from Ceará, and greatly admired his compatriot, José de Alencar. *Good Nigger* was designed, on one level, to publicize conditions Caminha had observed aboard the nation's fleet, but the novel's symbolic meaning goes far deeper. *Good Nigger*, whether consciously or unconsciously, transforms the optimism found in the structure and symbology of Alencar's *Iracema* into total despair.

In Alencar's Edenic legend, the native and the land were fused with Portugal and the sea, giving birth to Moacir, the new Brazil of the future. In Adolfo Caminha's text, Amaro – the "good nigger" of the title – is an immense black seaman, thrust from the harsh tortures of his past as a slave into the equally sadistic environment of the ship. He had dreamed of liberty and escape at sea, but the corvette on which he sails is as much a slave ship as the one described by Castro Alves – "a vast, apocalyptic bat" (Caminha, 1966:19). Amaro is happy at sea, despite the homosexual sadism of the ship's officers, for there he meets and falls in love with Aleixo, the innocent and beautiful white cabin boy. Amaro seduces Aleixo, but their union at sea cannot survive on land; Aleixo is again seduced, this time by Carolina, a syphilitic old Portuguese prostitute. The boy's loveless liaison with Carolina, as sterile as his relationship with Amaro, ends when the "good nigger" kills him in a fit of jealous rage. Thus Brazil, in Caminha's intensely pessimistic vision, is trapped between the degeneracy of its nonwhite population and the faded and sterile charms of Castro Alves's "great whore" of Europe and her immigrants.

By the opening years of the twentieth century, therefore, the Brazilian elite was desperately eager for any good news about the nation. Afonso Celso's best-selling primer for patriotism, *Why I'm Proud of My Country* (*Porque Me Ufano do Meu País*), published in 1901, tried to return to the optimism of the early Romantics and to the *ufanismo* of the first settlers. Celso preached that Brazil, with its "precious gifts" of landscape and climate, was the best of all possible worlds; its inhabitants should offer daily thanks to God for having made them Brazilians (1901:4).

There were also other, less traditional reasons for national pride. Large-scale European immigration had begun in 1886, and more than 2,700,000 foreigners had entered the country by 1914 (Skidmore, 1974:144); it was hoped that this large influx would make the nation whiter and, therefore, better. There were fine new buildings and boulevards in both Rio de Janeiro and São Paulo, where many of the new immigrants would settle, and such wondrous artifacts of progress as the automobile. The greatest national hero of the whole period, in fact, was Alberto Santos-Dumont, an expatriate who spent most of his life in Paris; his experiments with dirigibles and airplanes were proclaimed the highest expression of Brazilian intelligence, proof that the nation could indeed master the new technology.

Pessimism, however, was never far away. The enormous contradictions inherent in Brazilian attitudes toward the nation and its inhabitants are clearly visible in one of the most popular books of the period, Euclides da Cunha's fundamental *Rebellion in the Backlands* (*Os Sertões*), published in 1902. Da Cunha's analysis focused upon the revolt of Antônio the Counselor, a religious fanatic whose ragtag band of poorly armed followers had inflicted major and ignominious defeats on the forces of the Republic during 1896 and 1897. Da Cunha felt a certain sympathy for the rebels, the clear underdogs in this conflict in the interior of Bahia. Nonetheless, he saw the *sertão* area itself as barren and inhospitable and its native inhabitants as atavistic nonwhite barbarians, the products of a destructive miscegenation that, "in addition to obliterating the pre-eminent qualities of the higher race, serves to stimulate the revival of the primitive attributes of the lower" (1944:85).

Euclides da Cunha's assessment of the interior and its population was enormously influential. And though he was not at all certain of the final consequences of European immigration, many of his contemporaries saw his analysis as yet another argument in its favor. That immigration, however, turned out to be quite different from the Aryan triumph many members of the elite expected. Most of those who came to Brazil, particularly to São Paulo, were Italians, Spaniards, and Portuguese, all of whom sprang from the same supposedly inferior Mediterranean stock as the sad white colonists of Olavo Bilac's racial trinity. Moreover, it rapidly became clear that many of these immigrants had no intention of staying on the land, where they were supposed to take the place of even more inferior nonwhite laborers; they preferred to live in the city of São Paulo. The traditional land-owning aristocracy there began to realize that the city's industri-alization and the consequent growth of a new class of immigrant entrepreneurs might well represent a threat to its own power and prestige (Silva Brito, 1971:148-50). The immigrants were also blamed for bringing in the radical and dangerous new ideologies of socialism, communism, and anarchism: The first major strike in Brazil took place in São Paulo in 1917.

By the second decade of the twentieth century, only one ideal remained untainted by despair and uncertainty: technological progress. This idea was perhaps the most basic element in the formation of the first important new cultural movement in more than a generation, the movement that came to be known as Modernism. That movement, moreover, began in São Paulo, widely regarded as the most modern of Brazilian cities, "the model for Brazil today and a sample of the Brazil of the future" (in Silva Brito, 1971:153).

The "Week of Modern Art" the Modernists staged in São Paulo in 1922 is now perceived as the single most important happen-ing in twentieth-century Brazilian cultural history. It was the creation of a handful of young *paulista* intellectuals, no more than fifteen to twenty in number, who got permission to use the city's ornate Municipal Theater for three "festivals" of contem-porary art, music, and literature (Batista, Lopez, and Lima, 1972:395–8). These celebrations, held in February of 1922, were offered as an avant-garde, iconoclastic homage to the centenary of Brazilian independence. The Week was accompanied by dis-orders and scandal, all of which served the goal of Oswald de Andrade (1890–1954), the movement's permanent *enfant terrible* and one of the greatest public relations geniuses Brazil has pro-duced: to establish Modernism as the single viable alternative to the cultural status quo.

Despite its triumph in 1922, however, the movement faced several vital problems, problems that were never entirely resolved. One goal of the movement, as Mário de Andrade later described it, was modernity itself, "bringing the artistic intelligence of Brazil up to date" (1972a:242); some of the early poems the group produced are no more than paeans to the artifacts of urban progress: asphalt, skyscrapers, automobiles, and airplanes. At the same time, some of the Modernists – particularly Mário de Andrade – were conscious of the immense human costs of industrialization and urbanization, but it seemed impossible to separate the ideal of modernity from the artifact of the city itself.

The ideal of modernity was also inextricably linked to the presence of São Paulo's immigrant population. The movement as a whole was never able to develop a coherent position on immigration or on the broader question of European cultural influence. Foreign immigration meant modernization and industrialization, as well as a potential solution to the nation's racial inferiority, isolating nonwhites "like an island within the Caucasian race" (in Silva Brito, 1971:205). Many of the Modernists were simultaneously concerned, however, that their city, a crazy quilt of ethnic enclaves, no longer belonged to them.

This sense of personal alienation was intensified by a more general disquiet about the character of European culture. The Modernists were wildly enthusiastic about what little they knew of the literary and artistic avant-garde of France and Italy, but they had been profoundly shocked by the endless brutality of the World War. Alceu Amoroso Lima later wrote that this "vision of Europe, of all the world at war, brought us close to ourselves again. This war forced us to think about our own land, and with greater interest and affection" (1966:I, 84). The Modernists felt it their responsibility to build on this awareness, to find the real Brazil and sing its praises. Only in this way could they help to create a new national pride and unity, "to brazilianize the Brazilian, in the fullest sense; to make an antipatriotic nation patriotic" (Bandeira, 1958:II, 1093). This "brazilianizing" was to be accomplished, however, through artistic and literary efforts whose aesthetics and techniques were almost entirely drawn from those of contemporary Europe.

The Modernists' patriotic goal was undercut by their nearly total ignorance of the real Brazil, outside Rio de Janeiro and São

Paulo, and by the widespread belief – which the Modernists found implicit or explicit in much of what they read, and which they could not help but share – that Brazil's native-born inhabitants were generally inferior and incapable of progress. The Modernists loathed Olavo Bilac's Parnassian verses, but they tended to accept his vision of Brazil's three sad races almost without question. J. Pereira da Graça Aranha, the middle-aged patriarch of the movement, described the "ancient melancholy" of the Portuguese; the fears and self-deluding fantasies of the "rudimentary and formless" African mind, doomed to "perpetual childishness"; and the "metaphysics of terror," the primordial "fear that lies at the very beginnings of man's relationship with the Universe" that the Indian forever retains (1969:620–1). Paulo Prado's extremely influential *Portrait of Brazil* (*Retrato do Brasil*) of 1928 linked this national sadness to the unbridled sexuality he saw as characteristic of all three elements in the racial trinity. The result of rampant Indian, African, and Portuguese lust, Prado declared, was almost a medical certainty: "the development of a propensity to melancholy. *Post coitum animal triste, nisi gallus qui cantat*" (1944:107).

The Modernists, however, were also determined to crow, to discover and utilize a positive and cohesive national identity – the same goal the first Romantics had espoused almost a century before. Some members and allies of the group tried to idealize the colonial, Catholic past of the nation, but the Portuguese were not generally perceived as suitable symbols for a country that had just celebrated the centenary of its independence; they were also far too closely linked to the new colonizers of the twentieth century, the immigrants (Silva Brito, 1971:138–40). Black Brazilians provided an even less attractive image for the nation; their permanent inferiority was still widely perceived as a scientific fact. And, finally, the theory of degeneracy made it difficult to give serious consideration to all those Brazilians whose racial origins were tainted by miscegenation.

The solution that appears in many Modernist works was essentially that of the Romantics: escape into the past, away from the crowded streets of São Paulo to the shadowy forest pathways of Piratininga, the Indian village that once stood on the same site. As the Modernists sought the "itineraries" (*roteiros*) Oswald de Andrade demanded (1967:98) – to be both etiologies of the present and guidebooks to the future – they found the Tupi Indian world the best of a poor set of options. In fact, it appeared to be the only rational choice: "Tupi or not tupi, that is the question," Oswald declared in English (1967:95).[2]

Modernist "neo-Indianism," like its Romantic counterpart, was encouraged and made prestigious by the great enthusiasm for all things primitive and exotic among contemporary European intellectuals and artists. Nonetheless, the new "Indian fever" of the twentieth century owed a great deal to the national past, and its two basic currents were very much influenced by the attitudes and techniques of its great nineteenth-century predecessors.

The tone of Gonçalves Dias' Indianist poems was elegiac, lamenting the loss of the native world. The Indian past was discontinuous with the present, surviving only as a source of metaphors for events in the poet's personal life and in the contemporary history of the nation. Oswald de Andrade was rarely if ever elegiac; his tone was aggressive, sarcastic, and exaggerated. Yet Oswald's vision of the past was just as discontinuous as that of Gonçalves Dias: The Indian world was simply a series of possible metaphors for present and future options.

Oswald's "Brazil-Wood Manifesto" ("Manifesto da Poesia Pau Brasil") of 1924 took the sixteenth-century exportation of that wood, Brazil's first cash crop, as a metaphor for the new national culture the Modernists wanted to create, a culture based upon the exportation of ideas and styles rather than upon the old mania for importation in literature and art (1967:89–95). The 1928 "Anthropophagist Manifesto" ("Manifesto Antropófago"), Oswald's second primitivist creation, used a similar metaphor: The cannibalism of the natives served as the model for a different cultural relationship between Brazil and the outside world, one in which foreign influences would not be copied, but digested and absorbed as a precondition to the creation of a new, more independent national civilization (1967:95–103). Anthropophagism, of course, was also the kind of immense put-on Oswald greatly enjoyed; he tried to establish a new national chronology, which began with the consumption of Brazil's ill-fated first bishop, and terrified at least a few credulous souls by announcing that the first World Congress of Cannibals would be held in Brazil (Burns, 1968:66–7).

The most representative work in the other tradition of Modernist neo-Indianism, that faithful to the model of José de Alencar, is *Martim Cererê* (1928), Cassiano Ricardo's attempt to write a new national epic. In this work, as in *Iracema*, the past is not dead, but survives into the present; historical change is described as a function of human sexuality raised to the level of mythic fusion. The present is therefore a reproduction – in the fullest sense – of the past.

In both *Iracema* and *Martim Cererê*, the Indian world is reduced to a single telluric native maiden, who must be bedded by an equally mythologized Portuguese male in order to generate a new race, the Brazilians of the present. This act of miscegenation, both Alencar and Ricardo make clear, should be read as poetic symbol rather than anthropological fact. *Martim Cererê*, indeed, accomplishes a feat Alencar had not even attempted: to fuse the African with the other two races without implying sexual interaction between blacks and whites.

Martim Cererê was very popular when it appeared in 1928 and was in its fifth edition by 1936; it is still frequently hailed as one of the masterpieces of Modernism. Its popularity is in fact a function of its consciously unrealistic approach to the nation's history. No other Modernist production so effectively rewrote the past. Alencar had at least used Iracema's death and Moacir's name to suggest the human tragedy implicit in the conquest and destruction of the Indian world, but Cassiano Ricardo's poetic and intensely optimistic etiology managed to ignore or to transmute both that tragedy and the whole history of African slavery in Brazil.

The poem begins with its Iracema, the Uiara – the lovely water-spirit of the lakes and streams of the New World. Declaring that she is weary of the permanent sunshine of a tropical world that has never known darkness, the primeval world of the red-skinned "people of the dawn," she announces that she will marry only the warrior who can bring her the night. At this point a new race arrives: the Portuguese, the people of the sea, the white-skinned "people of mid-day." Martim – whose name is in part a reference to *Iracema* – is the handsomest of the Portuguese, and he falls madly in love with the Uiara. When he learns of the condition she has set for her marriage, the Portuguese ships bring night to her: the black-skinned "people of the night," the Africans.

The Uiara is thrilled with this wedding gift, and the happy couple is married – by the greatest of the early missionaries, José de Anchieta. This union produces three giant sons: one the color of the morning Sun, the nomad of the land and the preserver of primitive magic; one the color of the white heat of noonday, the nomad of the sea and the source of ambition; and one "darker than night" and therefore best able to endure the Sun of the tropics, whose contribution is the virtue of obedience. Together the three brothers put on seven-league boots and set out to explore the land and its riches (Ricardo, 1957:136–7). They and their heroic descendents unearth and exploit Brazil's mineral wealth and plant the hills of São Paulo with a new gold, coffee; the link between the past and present of the city is the cup of espresso coffee the poet sips (1957:203–4).

Martim Cererê represents nationalistic neo-Indianism triumphant. Paradoxically, however, the primitivism that was designed to unify the nation was accompanied by the gradual dissolution of the original Modernist group, which split into ever smaller, mutually hostile movements (Martins, 1969:92–102). Each new subgroup announced its existence and goals with manifestos, published its journals, and vigorously attacked its opponents.

There were several reasons for this fragmentation. First, the destruction of the old, Parnassian literary establishment, the primary goal of the early Modernists, was a far easier task than the construction of a new culture. Secondly, neo-Indianism, whatever its philosophical or ethnological trappings, implied a political vision – of aboriginal society and of the Brazil of the future that might be constructed upon that model. The increasing polarization of Brazilian politics around 1930 simply intensified differences in outlook and personality that already existed within Modernism. Oswald de Andrade, for example, allied himself with the Communist Party; Plínio Salgado, a lesser Modernist with close ties to Cassiano Ricardo, became the "National Chief" of Integralism, Brazil's fascist movement, and managed to combine admiration for Italy and Germany with the re-created Tupi war cries of his paramilitary "Green-Shirts" (Chasin, 1978). Within a few years, Modernism had become an idea rather than a coherent and cohesive movement, and almost anything written anywhere in Brazil – whatever its style, whatever its aesthetic or political ideology – was routinely classified as "Modernist."

As we look back, after more than half a century, the accomplishments of the original Modernists seem to have fallen far short of their stated goals. The legacy of the daring and brash young turks of São Paulo consists of a few outrageous public events and some fascinating manifestos and polemics, but not much real literature. The two most talented poets of the last fifty years, Manuel Bandeira and Carlos Drummond de Andrade, were not part of the original *paulista* group, and might well have developed their highly personal styles had Modernism never even existed.

São Paulo's Modernism, however, did have some positive and enduring consequences. Oswald de Andrade and his friends made literature fun and exciting and important once again. The Modernists introduced young Brazilian writers and artists to the major contemporary movements in European and North American culture. At the same time, the nationalistic ideology of Modernism – however vague and uninformed – encouraged serious study of Brazil's literary and artistic history, as well as of its popular culture. The movement also endeavored to transform both the vocabulary and the syntax of the literary language, to replace the classical Portuguese favored by the Academy of Letters with the lexicon and forms of the Brazilian vernacular. And although many of the works of the Modernists of São Paulo now seem no more than curious or amusing footnotes to the literary history of Brazil, the movement produced at least two books of lasting value. Mário de Andrade's *Hallucinated City* and *Macunaíma* combine modernity with tradition and offer a perspective on the personal and national implications of racial identity which is far more innovative and profound than that found in Ricardo's *Martim Cererê* or Oswald's Anthropophagism.

8

The harlequin:
Mário de Andrade

Mário de Andrade (1893–1945) was widely regarded in his own time as the "Pope" of Modernism. He vehemently rejected this title, but his position at the epicenter of the Modernist tumult has nonetheless remained a critical constant in the years since his death. There is general agreement today that Mário – through his learning, his personality, and his many activities – served as the intellectual focus of the Modernist generation and, in a very real sense, as its conscience.[1]

The intellectual content and seriousness of purpose of Mário's writings continue to attract critics and readers today, at a time when many of the elements of Modernism that appealed most strongly to Brazilians in the twenties – its aggressive humor, its immense if self-centered energy, its contradictory idealization of all things modern and all things Brazilian – seem terribly dated. By the end of his career, Mário had come to share this perception of the movement; he saw, more clearly than any other Modernist, that the revolution had too often turned into a boisterous and escapist party (1972a:238–41).

The general emphasis upon Mário's importance as a cultural presence, however, has tended to obscure his literary contributions. His writings, long praised but too often either misread or unread, have only recently begun to receive the attention they deserve. A number of Brazilian scholars have produced analyses of Mário's readings, his language and allusions, his poetics, and the evolution of his ideas about Brazil.[2] As a result, we know what most of the words mean, we know what Mário had read, and we have a fairly good idea of the poetic and fictive devices he utilized. Nonetheless, the reasoning behind Mário's language and techniques, the ultimate meaning of the works themselves, remains elusive.

Mário, then, is still presented as an important and highly talented intellectual whose tragically flawed works are too chaotic and too intensely personal to be deciphered and understood. Mário recognized, in his "Blues of a Difficult Writer" ("Lundu do Escritor Difícil"), that his works baffled and irritated readers. He insisted, however, that these were not valid reactions and that his texts, when placed within the proper context, were not impenetrable at all:

> I am a difficult writer,
> but look at who's to blame!...
> Everything hard can be easy
> if you just know the way.[3]

My intention here is to suggest another context, a new way of looking at Mário's works that can help us to understand the poems of *Hallucinated City* (*Paulicéia Desvairada*), published in 1922, and Mário's "rhapsody," *Macunaíma* (1928). This new interpretation begins with a simple statement of fact, but one that will distress and even anger his family and friends: Mário de Andrade must be read as a nonwhite writer. It is true that he came from an upper-middle-class family in São Paulo; his maternal grandfather had been a provincial governor, and his father was successful accountant (in Andrade, 1961:19–20). But Mário was, in fact, as much the genetic and somatic embodiment of the traditional racial trinity as Gonçalves Dias. Mário's skin color was the legacy of Indian ancestors; the contours of his nose and lips, so evident in photographs, portraits, and caricatures, were clearly African. Mário occasionally referred to his triple ancestry, and at least some of his friends and colleagues, aware of these nonwhite somatic traits, perceived his "mulatto character, expressed in his ostentatious toothiness," as an important element in Mário's position as a permanent "show" – the term is Oswald's – at the center of the Modernist festivities (in Alves, 1973:22).

We know very little about Mário's life, and even less about his private feelings regarding his ancestry and appearance. As I have suggested, there are a few overt and extremely important references in his works to his nonwhiteness, to his "soul spotted with races" (1972d:204). Nonetheless, a close reading of *Hallucinated City* and *Macunaíma* provides convincing evidence that Mário had thought seriously and originally about the problem of his own racial identity and about the parallel question of national identity, and that he endeavored to express his conclusions in his writings.

Perhaps the most fundamental theme in Mário's works is his own multiplicity, which derives from the absence of any single, unified personal identity. "I am three hundred, three hundred and fifty," he wrote, and though he hoped that "one day, at last, I'll bump into myself," that single self does not appear in his works (1972d:157). Mário rejected the commonplace idea that the three races were intermingled and fused, in Brazil or in his own being; he saw himself, rather, as multiple: simultaneously black, red, and white.

One can hypothesize several reasons for Mário's innovative elaboration of the idea of racial juxtaposition rather than fusion. First, fusion meant miscegenation, widely believed to lead to degeneracy. Mário appears to have been particularly sensitive to the term *mulato*, denoting miscegenation, which he sometimes employed in a pejorative sense to imply phoniness and dissimulation. The concept of racial fusion also seems to have disquieted him because it suggested to him the domination and potential destruction or absorption of one race by another. If no single identity could exist for Mário, it was vital for the separate and parallel racial selves to survive intact, balanced in an uneasy truce. He described the "sickness of America" – and, by extension, his own psychic malaise – as the result of the forcible domination of the African and Indian identities by a white self that had been strengthened and emboldened by external cultural and political influences as well as by European immigration (1972d:203–4).

The concept of parallel and multiple racial identities, existing simultaneously at a number of separate points on the continuum, also made it possible for Mário to believe that other, nongenetic identities could be added by education or taste. Thus he claimed that he was not only red and black and white, but French, as a result of his schooling; Italian, because of his love for music; North American, because he admired the United States; and so on (1972c:266). The simultaneous coexistence of these inherited and assumed identities was a comforting idea, one that could work to preserve him from the fear and self-doubt that marked other nonwhite Brazilian writers, but two critical problems remained: How could these separate and often contradictory identities be united, and how could they be utilized to produce literature?

Mário's solution was to try to submerge and unify his own multiplicity through identification with and description of far larger but equally multiple and contradictory collective entities: the city of São Paulo, in *Hallucinated City*; Brazil itself – and, by extension, all of South America – in *Macunaíma*. He described the composition of the first of these works as the direct result of an intense *comoção*, a word best translated not as "commotion," but as "shock," the shock of recognition and identification. He later used the same word to describe his first reactions when he encountered Macunaíma, "the hero without character," in a German anthropologist's collection of Amazonian Indian folktales (in Lopez, 1974:96).

The twenty-two poems of *Hallucinated City*, begun in the heat of a family argument, appear to have been written down rapidly, during a single week in December of 1920. Mário then drastically edited the manuscript, cutting it to half its original length. He finally read portions of it to a few astonished friends, but it is not clear that he intended to publish the work. Oswald de Andrade forced the issue, however, by quoting one poem in a 1921 article on Mário. As a result of this article, Mário lost many of his piano students, quarreled with his family, and was widely regarded as a lunatic (Silva Brito, 1971:228–35).

Reactions to the disjointed and fragmentary blank verse of the poem Oswald cited were so intense and so negative that Mário's friends persuaded him to write some sort of explanation to prove his sanity. When the full text of *Hallucinated City* was finally published, in July of 1922, it included a long introduction to which Mário gave the ironic, Machadian title "Extremely Interesting Preface." Although this carefully evasive explanation served as a basic text of Modernist poetics and introduced Brazilian readers to a number of contemporary European aesthetic theories, it was written well after the fact and refers to authors Mário probably had not yet read at the time he wrote the poems themselves. "I did not think about any of this" then, he declares, and he urges us not to take the preface too seriously; it is "not worth a damn," since he is not sure himself "where the *blague* leaves off and the serious begins" (1968a:18, 5).

Most critics have tended to start post facto, studying the ideas and techniques set forth in the "Extremely Interesting Preface" and then tracing their presence in the poems. It seems more useful, however, to reverse this process – to begin with the poetic text. The central image of that text is the harlequin, for Mário the primary "catalyst of associations" (Freitas Júnior, 1941:43).[4] The figure of the harlequin, with his suit of many colors, symbolizes both the contradictory diversity of São Paulo and the parallel multiplicity of the poet; it is, therefore, the basis for Mário's identification with the city.

The image of the harlequin, in the first edition of *Hallucinated City*, began with the volume's cover: a pattern of diamond-shaped lozenges of contrasting colors (Batista, Lopez, and Lima, 1972: 193). In his later "Improvisation on the Sickness of America" ("Improviso do Mal da América"), written in 1928, Mário made it clear that these colored lozenges referred to his own multiple racial identities, the red and white and black that "weave my harlequinate costume" (1972d:204). The harlequin also implies a pose – the madcap, apparently nonrational hilarity and essential marginality of the clown. But the evasive mask of carefree indifference Mário's harlequin wears hides the same sorrow and bitterness felt by Cruz e Sousa's "Acrobat of Pain": "And they say that clowns are happy!" Mário exclaims; "I never rattle the little bells in my harlequinate interior!. . ." (1968a:41)

The link between poet and city is the adjective *desvairada*, which appears in the volume's title. The word refers to the hallucinatory lunacy of the clown, induced by the city's multiplicity, and defines the superficially incoherent character of the text; it also means "disoriented" or "lost." The chaotic poems of *Paulicéia Desvairada* describe the poet's frenetic wanderings – his odyssey or *odisséia* – through the city of São Paulo, maddened by the juxtaposed contradictions of his own multiplicity; he describes himself, in fact, as "a Tupi Indian strumming a lute" (1968a:23). His goal is the discovery, within the city he loves, of a single, satisfying identity that will compensate for his own disunity. No such unity exists, however, for the city is itself lost, contradictory, harlequinate. The end of the search, therefore, is not identity, but identification in disunity.

If the poet is a racial harlequin, the harlequinate character of São Paulo is based upon Mário's perception of several orders of juxtaposed contradictions in its nature. The first order is climactic. The book's initial poem is preceded by a quotation from a classical Portuguese stylist, Friar Luís de Sousa: "Where even at the height of summer there were storms of wind and cold like unto the harshest winter" (1968a:21). The city's weather changes constantly, and the poems refer again and again to the sudden and violent shifts from light to mist, from heat to cold. These shifts are replicated within the poet, the city's troubador:

> The vernal seasons of sarcasm
> intermittently in my harlequinate heart...
> Intermittently...
> Other times it is a sick man, a chill
> in my sick soul like a long round sound...[5]

Additional contradictions can be found within the city, a crazy quilt of twentieth-century asphalt and primeval dust and mud, of conflicting architectural styles, of races and ethnic groups, of samba dancers and the Ballets Russes. At the heart of the city's disunity is its history. A few reminders of a more glorious past survive amid what Mário sees as the tawdry present of prostitutes, immigrants, politicians, and the cheap semiprecious stones of progress – a contrast that fills him with bitterness and a profound sense of loss. The Tietê River, once the route to the west of heroic pioneers, now trickles through a world of Italian social clubs and alien languages (1968a:32–3). The poet, reduced by time to the impotent jocularity of the harlequin, sits on a trolley and observes the city:

> But... behold, oh my eyes longing after yesterdays,
> that enchanted spectacle of the Avenue!
> Revive, oh ancestrally *paulista* gauchos!
> and oh horses of blood-red rage!
>
> Oranges, oranges, oranges!
> Avocados, cambucás and tangerines!
> *Guardate*! At the applause of the whizzing clown,
> heroic heir of that lordly race of pioneers,
> an immigrant's son elegantly passes by,
> blondly taming a motor car![6]

The two basic colors of São Paulo's harlequin costume are gold and gray – symbols, at one level, of climactic diversity: sunshine and mist, summer and winter. The same two colors are also used, however, to suggest a number of additional contradictions. The gold of the pioneer past has become the ash and smoke of the present, but the quest for gold remains a constant in the city's life, transformed into the capitalistic greed of the hated bourgeoisie and the "grand golden chorus of sacks of coffee!. . ." (1968a:75). The most damaging consequence of the new lust for gold is industrialization, the gray smoke of factories and the ashen faces of their tubercular workers. The land has been cheapened and changed beyond recognition: Cotton fields have become dance halls, rice paddies are now red-light districts, and the forests of banana trees have been replaced by joyless public parks dominated by the statuary of foreign cultures.

Stylistically, the poems of *Hallucinated City* were revolutionary; they appeared formlessly chaotic and utterly meaningless to many Brazilian readers in the twenties. Traditional meter and rhyme are absent, and the vocabulary includes created words and elements drawn from the nonpoetic lexicon of the machine. In a few instances, Mário was carried away by his emotions to shout and preach; it is also true that some of his references were so personal, so topical, that they can no longer be fully understood.

On the whole, however, the book has to be regarded as an enormous and innovative success. In the best poems, form and content merge, like the poet and his city. The lozenges of contradictory ideas and images are suddenly and outrageously juxtaposed, like the colors of the harlequin's costume; they are frequently stitched together by internal rhyme. Poetic and consciously antipoetic words and phrases collide like past and present, sun and rain; the languages of the city, as varied as its races and ethnic groups, are forced into coexistence. Thus São Paulo, the vast and contradictory "Gallicism crying in the wilderness of America," is portrayed through a text that is just as chaotic, just as alien, just as harlequinate – a strident shout in the cultural wasteland of pre-Modernist Brazil (1968a:20–1).

The "Extremely Interesting Preface" is something of a let-down after the poems of *Hallucinated City*. Its value is largely external, as a good-humored, reasonably clear, and very useful exposition of contemporary ideas about poetics and aesthetics, topics Mário later covered in greater detail in his 1925 *The Slave-Girl Who Is Not Isaura (A Escrava que não é Isaura)* (in 1972c:195–300). Much of the preface deals with questions that now seem either obvious or excessively topical – Mário's defense of free verse, for example. The preface, however, is also a brilliant demonstration of Mário's ability to avoid revelation as he hides behind a mask of verbiage and theory. There are no specific references to the book's central image of harlequinate diversity and conflict, an image drawn from the poet's own racial multiplicity. Moreover, because the most obvious stylistic technique in the poems – the juxtaposition of contradictory and discordant elements – might lead readers to perceive the personal implications of the text, Mário cleverly uses allusion and misdirection to create the complicated theory (which he openly admits is nonsensical) of melodic, harmonic, and polyphonic verse (1968a:11–15).

During the three years following the publication of *Hallucinated City*, Mário came to realize that "São Paulo is not the only harlequinate city" in Brazil (1972d:131). The best poem of this period, the 1923 "Carnival in Rio" ("Carnaval Carioca"), provided a new tool, metamorphosis, which could be used to express that diversity. In *Hallucinated City*, the various parallel identities of poet and city coexisted in concrete, immutable form – the multicolored lozenges of the harlequin's suit. In "Carnival," each participant in the festivities can move from one potential identity to another, from one lozenge to another, simply by changing costume. Thus the dancers – even the most extreme case and the focus of Mário's poem, the male cashier who transforms himself into a sexy Bahian girl – do not become what they are not, but what they also, simultaneously, are (1972d:110–21).

By 1925 Mário had become convinced that it was his responsibility to try to create a single literary work that would sum up Brazil's diversity. He prepared for this task by reading every-

thing he could find, endeavoring to transform himself intellectually, to move from the dominant identity of urban whiteness
implicit in his education to another potential identity, based
upon his nonwhiteness, that would be more truly Brazilian. In
the second volume of *Vom Roroima zum Orinoco*, by the German
anthropologist Theodor Koch-Grünberg, Mário discovered a series of native folktales dealing with the exploits of Macunaíma,
the culture hero and trickster of one Amazonian tribe (Koch-
Grünberg, 1924).

Mário immediately felt the intense *comoção* of self-recognition,
and decided to use the character of Macunaíma, the "hero without character," as the central figure in a long prose text. The
hero's lack of character functions at two levels, ethical and national: He is inconsistent and amoral in his actions; and his
harlequinate lack of any fixed racial or cultural identity is that of
Brazil as a whole, still formless and without "either a civilization
of its own or a traditional sense of self," in Mário's words (in
Lopez, 1974:87). Macunaíma, moreover, is more South American than Brazilian; he is born where Guyana and Venezuela meet
Brazil, and his travels take him from the Amazon to the Andes
to the pampas of Argentina.

Mário claimed to have written the first draft of *Macunaíma* during a single week in December of 1926 (in Lopez, 1974:90), but
that draft was based upon several years of intensive ethnographic
and linguistic research, and was drastically revised before publication in 1928. He produced several different prefaces to the text,
but decided not to publish any of them; he also referred to *Macunaíma*
in his correspondence and in articles (in Lopez, 1974:87–102). All
of these explanations and justifications, however, are as contradictory and evasive as the "Extremely Interesting Preface." Mário
sometimes claimed, for example, that there were no symbols in
the text, but his 1943 analysis of the role of Vei – his only detailed
explication of any portion of the book – reveals a tightly structured allegorical symbolism (in Lopez, 1974:101–2).

What are we to make of these contradictions? I believe, first,
that *Macunaíma* was far more personal than Mário was ever pub-

licly willing to admit, and that this is one reason for the evasiveness of his accounts of its composition and meaning. Secondly, although the text is a highly conscious creation, the product of hundreds of hours of research and rewriting, we must also accept Mário's assertion that the final utilization of the materials he had collected was in large measure determined by his subconscious, which created symbolic relationships and meanings he had not planned (in Lopez, 1974:101).

Mário was enormously excited when he finished the final draft of *Macunaíma* in 1927, astonished at what his learning and his unconscious mind had combined to create. He was therefore shocked and embittered by the almost universally negative reactions of his contemporaries. The book was harshly criticized, by other Modernists as well as by older writers whose opinions Mário respected; to make matters worse, the text was published shortly after the "Anthropophagist Manifesto," and some readers appear to have been convinced that Mário had simply put Oswald's theory into practice. Mário frequently complained that no one had ever understood the text that he regarded as his masterpiece, and finally concluded that it had been a failure (1966:330).

It is easy to feel sympathy for Mário's distress, but the reactions of his readers are understandable. *Macunaíma* is written in an artificial and extremely difficult language, Mário's own invention, which combines popular syntax with a lexicon drawn from a number of native and foreign languages as well as from every regional dialect within Brazilian Portuguese. The structure of *Macunaíma*, moreover, appears as chaotic as its language – a formless series of utterly illogical events. The book is also obscene; many of Mário's contemporaries were shocked by what they viewed as pure pornography, but even the book's Rabelaisian bawdiness appears pointless. In addition, large sections of *Macunaíma* are found texts, sometimes copied almost word for word from Koch-Grünberg and other collectors of Brazilian Indian folktales, which have been tossed together without any obvious logic. When Mário was accused, rather gently, of plagiarism, he admitted, "I copied everybody," but also insisted, "I made things up whenever I felt like it and, above all, whenever I needed to make sure that my creation would remain art and not the dry documentation of scholarship" (in Lopez, 1974:99, 94).

I believe, however, that this biography of the "hero without character," if read as I am convinced Mário consciously and unconsciously intended it to be, is not a failed text but one of the two or three greatest works of Brazilian literature – the high point in a long national tradition but also a work far ahead of its time, the independent precursor of what is now generally described as the "magic realism" of the Spanish-American novel of the fifties and sixties (Rodríguez Monegal, 1977:109–12). And, finally, despite its riotously funny and often scatological humor, Mário's text is perhaps the most profoundly tragic work in Brazilian literature, a native *Don Quijote*.

The complexity of this utterly untranslatable book begins with its genre. It has often been classified as a novel – sometimes, most erroneously, as a picaresque novel – although Mário never referred to it as such. The book was first advertised as a *história*, a term that combines the historical context of the text and its folkloric origins as a story. When it was published, the title page defined it as a *rapsódia*, another term with a double meaning. In music, a rhapsody is a light diversion, a variation using popular national themes; in literature, it is the creation of the rhapsodist, the personification, in Mário's definition, of a tradition that flowed directly from the ancient bards of pre-Homeric Greece to the oral literature of northeastern Brazil in the twentieth century. The function of the rhapsodist, Mário declared, remained the transformation of contemporary and historical events into authentic literary expressions of the popular mind (in Lopez, 1974:98–9).

Mário's rhapsodic text – the story of Macunaíma's origins in the Amazonian forests, his trip to São Paulo, and his return to the jungles before he ascends into the heavens to become the Big Dipper – is far less chaotic than several generations of critics have claimed. Though it does not have a standard novelistic framework, the rhapsody is quite rigidly organized around a series of complex internal structures that are symbolic or allegorical in content. These structures, perhaps most usefully described as codes, are both the source of *Macunaíma*'s multiplicity and apparent incoherence and the key to its meaning.[7] It is worthwhile, therefore, to deconstruct the text in order to look closely at several of the codes that coexist within it.[8]

The chronological and cosmogonic codes

In *Macunaíma*, what we call time, the fixed chronology of civilization, exists only within the calendars and clocks of São Paulo. Time outside the city is multiple and simultaneous, like the harlequinate juxtapositions of past and present in *Hallucinated City*. Thus the chronology of the real world of São Paulo in the twenties coexists with all of Brazilian history and with a primitive vision of multiple and parallel chronologies, of worlds being created and destroyed.

The multiplicity of time is a function, in fact, of the multiple character of the universe, which exists simultaneously at various stages of development and in which there are few fixed forms: Humans become plants, mountains, and waterfalls; animals and insects were once human; machines were once animals, and people can become machines; the Moon and stars are still being created, formed of birds and snakes and human beings.

This cosmogonic multiplicity and simultaneity is the basis for the magic metamorphoses that take place within the text. The hero, in part because he has no fixed character of his own, realizes that every identity carries within it a series of other potential identities: those which once existed and those which may yet come to be – a more elaborate form of Mário's vision of "Carnival in Rio." Magic simply involves moving oneself or others from one identity to another. Thus, to give but one example, the hero is magically and instantly transformed from infant to adult, a metamorphosis possible because the hero's adult identity is already implicit within the child, the father of the man. Only Macunaíma's head remains baby-sized; it is also rhomboid – the diamond shape of the lozenges in the harlequin's suit (1972b:22).

The petrological code

The opposite of metamorphosis is petrification – the irreversible foreclosure of potential options for existence as the multiple identities become forever fixed in a single, often ironic form. Macunaíma uses this implicit petrous identity as the basis for some of his magic: He turns a visiting Englishman into the stone structure of the London Bank; when Macunaíma leaves São Paulo to return to the forest, he looks back, like Lot's wife, and changes the whole bustling metropolis into an enormous stone sloth (1972b: 131, 177).

Stones retain some trace of their original identities, however, and this is the basis for the power of the *muiraquitã*, the magic talisman that Ci, the Empress of the Forests and the Queen of the Amazon Women, gives to Macunaíma before she ascends into the heavens. The hero quickly loses the stone, and his journey to São Paulo to recover it from the villain, Venceslau Pietro Pietra, forms the major portion of the plot. Macunaíma finally kills Pietra and regains the *muiraquitã*, but he loses it a second time at the end of the book and gives up on the world. Pietra is a foreigner, a Peruvian-Italian trader, and is used on one level to satirize São Paulo's immigrants and their pretensions. The conflict between the hero and Pietra is not, however, a simple allegory for the native–foreigner dialectic; the trader is also, simultaneously, the evil giant Piamã – Macunaíma's traditional foe in native folklore. Pietra-Piamã, therefore, is a universal symbol of evil, combining the sins of greed and of sacrilege in his mania for collecting stones – the petrified remains of animals, of human beings, even of entire civilizations. This obsession is implicit in the giant's Italian name (1972b:64–5).

Macunaíma is too free a spirit to contain a petrous identity within his multiplicity. At the end of the book, the Tupi Indians have all been petrified; a gigantic stone turtle, their traditional totemic animal, is all that remains of their race. The hero writes his own epitaph upon its surface – "I DID NOT COME INTO THIS WORLD TO BE A STONE!" – and departs to become the Big Dipper (1972b:215–17).

The celestial code

Superior, nonpetrous spirits can rise, like Macunaíma, to become stars – an idea Mário took from Indian mythology. Their ascent is proof of their basic goodness, but the stellar option also represents frustration, sorrow, and evasion; it is, in fact, as much a final, irreversible fixation of identity as is petrification. Thus Iriqui, one of the wives of Mucunaíma's brother Jiguê, becomes a star in the Pleiades when she can no longer attract the hero. When their infant son dies, Macunaíma's wife Ci transforms herself into Beta Centauri (1972b:188, 32).

The heavens contain other symbols. Macunaíma endeavors, during his stay in São Paulo, to teach the city's inhabitants the true nature of the universe, the real and multiple identity of all things. Perhaps his greatest single good deed, within the context of the text, is that he saves the *paulistas* from the false and banal cosmography of the state. The hero ridicules the national stellar symbol, the Southern Cross, and shows his audience that the constellation is really the final transformation of Pauí-Pódole, the Father of the Curassows, the first and greatest of that species of birds. This revelation so moves the sophisticated and cosmopolitan *paulistas* that they become as little children, and go back to their homes afraid that they will wet their beds during the night (1972b:114–17).

Another aspect of the celestial code, which Mário himself explained in 1943, is the relationship between the hero and Vei, the feminine Sun. Vei intends that Macunaíma, as Brazil, should marry one of her daughters; the nation would thereby attain its potential identity as a great tropical civilization, like ancient Egypt and Mexico. The hero, however, wanders off to fornicate with a Portuguese girl, causing Vei to change her mind. Vei gets her revenge at the very end of the text, when she warms the hero's body to rekindle his dormant lust. As a result, Macunaíma dives into a lake to copulate with a seductive water-spirit, the Uiara; a swarm of piranhas devour most of his body, he loses the *muiraquitã* again, and he decides to abandon the Earth for life among the stars (1972b:86–91, 211–15).

The entomologic code

Mário uses insects to establish and describe the ideal relationship between primitive man and his environment. Man is master of the insect world, and primitive society is built around a
series of vital insect-centered rituals of human interaction: shooing
away mosquitoes, searching for ticks, picking lice. This ancient
relationship breaks down in São Paulo. Suzi, the city girl who is
Jiguê's third wife, utterly deforms ritual by picking her own lice,
an act symbolizing the shift from primitive communality to urban
individualism, from public virtue to private vice. She even takes
off her head of hair in order to find the insects more efficiently,
thereby deforming nature as well (1972b:155–8). Macunaíma also
realizes that ants are literally taking over São Paulo and Brazil.
The image of the vast urban ant hill was a Modernist commonplace and appears in *Hallucinated City*, but the hero's preoccupation is now concrete rather than metaphoric: The insect world is
escaping from civilized man's control. Macunaíma cannot save
modern Brazil from its ants, nor can he restore the traditional
model of symbiosis and respect. He can only warn Brazilians,
through his famous dictum, "TOO MANY ANTS AND TOO
LITTLE HEALTH: / SUCH IS THE SICKNESS OF BRAZIL"
(1972b:89, 105, 208).

The epidemiological code

There is, it appears, no disease in the forests where the hero is
born. São Paulo's grayness, in *Hallucinated City*, is related to its
diseases, laryngitis and tuberculosis. The São Paulo Macunaíma
enters is filled with a far greater assortment of diseases, and he
catches almost all of them: erysipelas, scarlet fever, thrush, mea-
sles, and so on. Precisely because he has never really grown up,
he is particularly susceptible to the illnesses of civilized children.
The hero, moreover, perceives that disease is an integral part of
the city's life; the monstrous animal-machines that sweep the
streets, for example, are designed to stir up bacteria and thereby
kill enough people to stabilize the population (1972b:103).

Macunaíma is no more healthy when he leaves São Paulo to return to the forest. His diseases simply become more tropical, providing etiologies for such ailments as malaria and leprosy. He finally becomes not merely the victim of disease but its active agent, as he consciously infects Jiguê with the leprosy that will destroy his entire family. Only Macunaíma escapes this disease, but its effects are symbolically repeated in his final maiming by the piranhas.

The ornithological code

Birds have two vital functions within the text. First, they provide continuity for the plot, reflecting the transformations of the hero. Macunaíma's nobility – as Ci's husband, he becomes Emperor of the forests and ruler of the single-breasted Amazons – and his original integration into the natural world are symbolically represented by the bright canopy of parrots that always flies above his head. When he enters São Paulo – a world in which the riches of the forest are almost worthless, quickly dissipated on lobsters, champagne, and prostitutes – the parrot canopy flies away.

The birds return only when the hero goes back to the forest, protecting him from the heat of vengeful Vei, but he has changed and they slowly begin to drift away. He barely notices, for he now cares only about the two chickens he has brought back from São Paulo – helpless, flightless birds without function in the forest (1972b:177). Macunaíma is no longer attracted to Iriqui, one of Jiguê's Indian wives, and part of his imperial canopy goes with her to form the Pleiades. The rest depart when he betrays and infects his brothers with leprosy. Only one parrot remains to converse with Macunaíma, to witness his ascension into the sky, and to teach the hero's language and deeds to a stranger and, thereby, to us. The parrot then flies away, like Machado's Tristão and Fidélia, to find a new life in Portugal.[9]

The ornithological code is also the primary source of one of the most important concepts in the book, the archetypal model – the Pódole – of every living species. The Pauí-Pódole, the Father of the Curassows, has left his descendents behind on earth, and is now what Brazilians incorrectly call the Southern Cross. As a result of Macunaíma's mindless treachery, toward the end of the text, Jiguê is devoured by leprosy and becomes the ghost leper that infects and digests the oldest brother, Maanape, and the beautiful princess who is their companion. The multiple, all-consuming ghost then attacks the Father of the Vultures, the archetypal king vulture, and receives a new identity as the bird's second head (1972b:203).[10] The Father of the Vultures does not join the Father of the Curassows in the heavens, however; the world of the forest is dying, and scavengers must remain to feed upon it and thereby purify it.

The code of the machine

When Macunaíma first encounters the city of São Paulo, he is astonished by its machines, artifacts he can comprehend only in terms of the natural world he knows. He adapts quickly to this new environment, however, because he perceives that the multiplicity and potentiality of his cosmogonic vision still apply to modern man and his machines. After pondering the question, he concludes that "the men were in fact machines and the machines were in fact men" (1972b:52). Once this multiple and simultaneous identity is established, Macunaíma can extend the magic of metamorphosis to this new order, turning his brother Jiguê into a telephone whenever he needs to make a call.

The hero, in another of his rare good deeds, transmits his perception of technology as merely one of the potential identities of nature to a chauffeur – a social type described, in one of Mário's most important nonfolkloric sources, as the prototype of the new man of the twentieth century, the "technicalized savage" who is the master of the machine (Keyserling, 1927:229). In a replication of the Southern Cross incident, Macunaíma tells a chauffeur and his girlfriend the story of the jaguar who became the first automobile and of her vast, sexually differentiated litter of male Fords and female Chevrolets. The authenticity of this etiology provides the chauffeur with a tradition rooted in the real Brazil, leaving him and the girl speechless and in tears (1972b:167–70).

The hero, however, is also tempted by the machine – a word he extends to include all manufactured articles. Vei gives him the *vatá*, the magic fire stone, but this most precious of objects in the forest is of no interest in a world of matches and lighters, and Macunaíma trades it away to get his picture in the papers (1972b:91). When he leaves São Paulo, he takes with him two of its artifacts: a Smith-Wesson revolver and a Pathek watch. These objects are as useless in the forest as his chickens, but Macunaíma clings to these artificial talismans during his last days on Earth, managing to recover them from the piranhas and take them with him up to the heavens. The *muiraquitã*, the real talisman, is lost forever.

The racial code

Macunaíma, like Mário's harlequin, is at once black and red and white: He is born a black-skinned Indian, but becomes white, blond, and blue-eyed when he bathes in the water that fills a footprint left by Saint Thomas. In a standard folk etiology of racial diversity, the hero so muddies the water that Jiguê, who bathes second, becomes a red-skinned Indian; even less water is left for Maanape, who can only lighten his palms and the soles of his feet. In this symbolic baptism, Jiguê and Maanape, previously no more than foils for the hero's childish pranks, acquire definition as independent personalities; but their new forms, as the Indian and the African, are simply personifications of two somatic and cultural identities already implicit in Macunaíma the harlequin.

Maanape is the sorcerer, a symbol of the survival of African religion and magic in Brazil; it is he who cures the hero's many urban diseases. Once the three brothers leave São Paulo to return to the Indian forests, Maanape becomes a lost and alien figure without function; he cannot even cure his own leprosy.

Jiguê the Indian is braver than Macunaíma, but he is not very intelligent, particularly where women are concerned. He comes into his own, however, when the brothers reenter the forest. As the hero's sexual appeal and potency fade, the pattern of seduction is reversed; it is Jiguê who beds the beautiful princess who would seem to be Macunaíma's natural mate. Jiguê also retains the ancestral Indian magic of hunting and fishing, which Macunaíma literally throws away in mindless fits of jealous impotence (1972b:193–6). The alienated envy of the tragically whitened and weakened hero leads him to infect Jiguê with leprosy, thereby destroying his companions and his own future on earth.

The sexual code

Macunaíma is born lustful and moves magically from infantile sexuality to adult potency. He seduces all three of Jiguê's wives, and has three other important sexual relationships – with Ci, with the anonymous princess, and with the Uiara. He also tries to bed every female he meets, and generally succeeds, at least until the final chapters of the text.

The sexuality that pervades *Macunaíma* has several important and related functions. First, it provides a metaphor for the primitive–urban dialectic: Sex is freely given and taken among the Indians, but Macunaíma usually has to pay for it in São Paulo, a fact that astonishes and puzzles him. Fascinated by the city's prostitutes – most of whom are foreign and all of whom claim to be French – and by their use of such machine-made aids to seduction as rouge and lipstick, the hero transforms himself into a French whore, with banana stalks for breasts, and tries to seduce Pietra in order to regain the *muiraquitã* (1972b:62–6). The attempt fails when Pietra gets too physical, but the episode is the first hint that Macunaíma, in the city, is slowly losing his masculinity; by the time he returns to the forest, he is so asexual that the monster Mapinguari, who likes only girls, pursues him by mistake (1972b:181).

Sex in *Macunaíma* is often extremely violent. The hero's sexual encounters with Jiguê's first two wives, Sofará and Iriqui, involve mutual flagellation and mutilation, elements replicated in his final copulation with the Uiara. Macunaíma rapes Ci violently, while his brothers hold her down, and their sexual relationship after marriage is frequently and graphically sadomasochistic (1972b:27–30).[11] All of this sexual aggression is meaningful, within the context of the text, because it emphasizes that sex is power, and that Macunaíma's gradual impotence is merely a metaphor for the dissipation of his primitive powers that results from his contact with the white, urban world of São Paulo.

The link between sex and power is most explicit in the episode of the *macumba* ("voodoo") ritual in Rio, a tangle of inverted sexual identities and the most brutal and terrifying section of the text. The ceremony calls up Exu, the male African deity of evil, who takes over the body of a fat Polish whore. As Macunaíma copulates with the whore possessed by Exu, it becomes clear that the hero is really Exu's son, and is therefore fornicating with his own father. As a reward for Macunaíma's sexual prowess, Exu works sympathetic magic: The hero beats and tortures the whore's body in a fit of almost incomprehensible sadism, but all her wounds are transferred to the body of Pietra in São Paulo – Macunaíma's first victory over his great adversary (1972b:73–82).

This sexual sadomasochism also symbolizes Macunaíma's destiny as a destructive rather than a creative force. A web of allusions and symbols make it clear that the hero's exaggerated natural sexuality reflects one supreme potential identity within his multiplicity – as the procreator of a race, as a Pódole. Thus Macunaíma's first liaison, with Sofará, refers to the cosmogony implicit in the ending of Alencar's *The Guarani Indian*: Sofará, in Indian legend, was the wife of the only man to survive the Deluge, and is therefore the mother of mankind. Jiguê sends Sofará home to her father, short-circuiting the generative potential of her identity (Proença, 1977:129, 298). The same possibility exists in Macunaíma's relationship with Iriqui, who is described in terms that suggest Alencar's Iracema, but she rises to the Pleiades without bearing children. The episode of the hero's marriage to Ci, the Mother of the Forest and another Iracema figure, is more promising, for a child is born, a new Moacir. The Edenic potential is destroyed when the infant dies and Ci also departs for the heavens.

Macunaíma, weakened and contaminated by the modernity of São Paulo, is still obsessed with sex, but his generative potential is forever eliminated during his stay there. He has lost so much of his native cunning that a monkey easily tricks him into smashing his own testicles with a rock (1972b:147–8). The shock kills Macunaíma, but Maanape brings him back to life and gives him a pair of coconuts as substitutes. The hero's ability to serve as a Pódole, however, is lost. He becomes a voyeur, observing the lovemaking of the chauffeur and his girl. Once back in the forest, the hero gradually loses all interest in sex, even with the beautiful princess; his encounter with the Uiara is the last, artificially induced spasm of lust, and the piranhas devour his coconuts.

The linguistic code

Mário sought to use the artificial language in which *Macunaíma* is written to "deregionalize" the nation, to unify Brazilian Portuguese by juxtaposing words taken from every regional dialect. The language is also intended to suggest that the text itself refers to the nation as a whole rather than to any single area. In addition, loan words from European languages coexist with Africanisms and borrowings from a number of native Indian tongues to form the harlequinate lexicon of the text. Enumeration, one key technique in Mário's effort to unify Brazil linguistically through *Macunaíma*, has greatly puzzled and irritated readers. These long intercalated lists of synonyms drawn from a number of dialects – words for "fish" or "parrot," for example – nonetheless serve two functions: to make the book, and its author, more truly and completely Brazilian; and to present nonmeaningful tone poems, brief melodic interludes of sounds and rhythms that reproduce the rhapsodist's accompaniment on the lyre, gusla, or guitar.

Macunaíma begins to talk rather late in his brief childhood, but he is as fascinated by language as Mário. When he goes to

São Paulo, he tries – like a new Adam in a concrete Eden – to give names to what he sees, juxtaposing the natural and the mechanical: The marmoset-elevator climbs up the palm-tree-building, for example. He also uses, or at least pretends to use, the city's alien languages: English, French, and Italian. He is most intrigued, however, by a more curious linguistic phenomenon, the almost total discontinuity between what Brazilians say and what they write, between the spoken language and formal, pretentious written Portuguese.

Macunaíma masters this alien second tongue and writes the long "Letter to the Amazons" in it, asking for more funds and showing off what he has learned (1972b:95–108). The letter is a delightful linguistic *tour de force*, combining meaningless quotations from the classics, grammatical over-correction, bureaucratic discourse, and pompous allusions that are often not quite exact. This brilliant satire on the traditional reactions of foreign travelers to Brazil, from Pêro Vaz de Caminha on, is also an attack on the ignorance implicit in the high-flown, verborrheic style every educated and semieducated Brazilian, in Mário's view, dreamed of mastering.

The hero's ability to use this style, however, is also evidence of his transformation and contamination by the urban civilization of policemen, whores, and politicians he praises in this letter. As he adopts this obsolete and dysfunctional language, he begins to lose his own tongue and his own identity. Thus, for example, it is thanks to Macunaíma's influence that the *paulistas* learn to replace an imported gallicism, *boutonnière*, with an authentic native term, *puíto*, an Indianism for "anus." This is one of the hero's minor accomplishments in a series of conscious or unconscious efforts to give the city's inhabitants their Brazilian roots, but Macunaíma is later startled when a German girl offers to put a flower in his *puíto*, and at first does not understand her (1972b:112–13).

Macunaíma is also increasingly fixated upon obscenity, upon just plain talking dirty. This fixation is symbolic of his gradual loss of sexual potency, the substitution of language for action.

And, like Mário himself, the hero becomes a collector of words. When he sees Pietra's collection of stones – concrete and potentially powerful artifacts, past beings and civilizations in petrified form – Macunaíma is tempted to start one of his own. He decides, however, that it sounds like too much work, and makes up his mind to gather words rather than things; he amasses a vast repertoire of dirty words from every language and every country. Macunaíma attempts to use the words against Pietra, but the giant is intrigued rather than frightened or insulted; a few drops of rain have a far greater effect upon the enemy than all of the hero's obscenities, which are as ultimately useless as Mário's careful collection of regional synonyms (1972b:69–70, 128–30). And, in the final destruction of Macunaíma's tribe and world, language itself is lost. The mute hero rises to the silence of the heavens; his language and that of his tribe, no longer used by humans, is preserved only in the rote memory of a parrot.[12]

If we now reconstruct the text, reintegrating these separate codes, it becomes clear that Mário managed to combine within it the two traditional functions of Indianism: etiology, explaining the present; and elegy, mourning the loss of the past while finding lessons in it for the present. Macunaíma is a genuine culture hero, both in his folkloric origins and in his role within Mário's text. It is through him that an incredibly diverse series of natural and social phenomena are explained: why the Moon and stars exist, why the Sun is yellow, where automobiles come from, why Brazil has soccer, soft drinks, and obscene gestures. The hero and his brothers also explain Brazil's racial diversity: It is a nation that was once primarily Indian and African, that has been whitened by Christianity but remains, simultaneously and harlequinately, white and red and black.

The etiological function of *Macunaíma*, however, includes the explanation of negative national characteristics, a departure from the optimism of Alencar. Brazilians had long perceived their nation and its culture as not yet fully formed, not yet adult. Macunaíma is indeed both infant and man, for he never grows up; the magic of the agouti rodent gives him the body of an adult, but his head – the seat of intelligence and sensibility – remains small and deformed, with the "nauseating baby face of a child" (1972b:22). This transformation, like all of the hero's other metamorphoses, also reflects Brazil's lack of a fixed and true identity.

Although Macunaíma fulfills his etiological function, he utterly fails to live up to his creative potential as an authentic culture hero, one who not only explains the present but also, as a Pódole, preserves the past and engenders the future. That failure, the central theme of the text, moves *Macunaíma* beyond the tradition of Alencar. The book is not only an etiological myth of national creation, but an explanation of the annihilation of the future, a myth of national destruction. Macunaíma is the Brazil that might have been: the creative, balanced coexistence of the three races within a culture rooted in the traditions of the past, conscious of the potential of its multiplicity, and destined to flourish as a great tropical civilization. When the mutilated and impotent hero departs for the heavens, still clutching his chickens, his watch, and his revolver, he leaves no descendants; his tribe – and Brazil's future – vanishes. All that remains is the world of ants and machines and disease, the city of stone and its petrous inhabitants.

The text, therefore is elegiac, mourning the lost future as well as the lost past. Mário may well have hoped that there was still time to unify Brazilians through the language and allegory of his text, to warn them of the perils of sterility, disease, and dependency. These goals help explain Mário's bitter despair when his warning was criticized and misunderstood. But *Macunaíma* is also, I believe, a very personal document, as much a journal of life on the continuum as the works of Gonçalves Dias, Machado, or Cruz e Sousa. Through the hero, Mário seeks to identify himself with the real Brazil – and, in fact, with the whole of Latin America. His own identity, like that of the nation and the continent, is harlequinate and multiple, and must remain so. Mário's "Improvisation on the Sickness of America," written a few months before *Macunaíma* was published, describes the greatest of all the ailments afflicting him and the nation, and one that Macunaíma shared: the disease of whiteness that is slowly destroying the other racial identities that color both his harlequin's suit and his soul, foreclosing his multiple options for existence on the racial continuum.

Even as he wrote his rhapsodic text, Mário de Andrade appears to have feared that his warning might go unheeded. All he had to offer Brazilians were his words, words that, as Macunaíma discovers, are less powerful than a few drops of rain. Moreover, those who might have understood and heeded his message – those Brazilians not yet contaminated by cultural dependency, those who still retained tradition and racial and cultural diversity – could not read. Despite all of Mário's efforts to nationalize the vocabulary and syntax of his text, it is as pointless as the ridiculous letter Macunaíma writes to the illiterate Amazons – a text to which there can be no reply. Those who attempt the impossible task of saving Brazil from modernity and whiteness by endeavoring to show the nation its roots and by celebrating its harlequinate racial diversity may, like Macunaíma, escape petrification as "mute statues in the corners of public gardens a hundred years from now," as Mário wrote of himself in 1936 (in Pinheiro Machado, 1976:100). The fate that awaits them, however, is the same evasive fixation of identity the frustrated and despairing hero chooses in the end: "the useless brilliance of the stars" (in Lopez, 1972:56) – a destiny Mário de Andrade assigned to José de Alencar, and a destiny he also predicted for himself.[13]

Conclusion:
The Edenic metaphor

In the decade following the unheeded warning of Mário de Andrade's *Macunaíma*, many members of the Brazilian elite – particularly in the South – became convinced that the triumph of whiteness Mário had described as the "sickness of America" was almost complete. João Pandiá Calógeras declared, in 1930, that "the heritage of Ham is dissolving" (1939:30), and the 1940 census did provide concrete evidence of the comforting whiteness of society in southern Brazil: The population of the state of São Paulo was classified as almost 85 percent white, with only 7 percent defined as black and less than 5 percent as of mixed race (*pardos*) (Smith, 1963:70). By 1943 Fernando de Azevedo could confidently conclude:

If we admit that Negroes and Indians are continuing to disappear, both in the successive dilutions of white blood and in the constant process of biological and social selection, and that immigration, especially that of a Mediterranean origin, is not at a standstill, the white man will not only have in Brazil his major field of life and culture in the tropics, but be able to take from old Europe – citadel of the white race – before it passes to other hands, the torch of western civilization to which the Brazilians will give a new and intense light – that of the atmosphere of their own civilization. [1950:40–1]

The final victory of white Brazil did not seem nearly so certain in other areas of the nation, particularly in the Northeast. The same census defined the population of the state of Bahia as less than 27 percent white; blacks (20 percent) and *pardos* (51 percent) were far more numerous (Smith, 1963:70). This uncertainty was reflected in the ambiguities of the regional literature of the North-

east – in the "New Novel" of the area, which began to appear
around 1928, and in the historical studies and social theories of
Gilberto Freyre.

José Américo de Almeida, the patriarch of the "New Novel,"
provided a link between twentieth-century regional fiction and
the traditions of literary abolitionism and Naturalism. The Naturalist novel was *passé* in the South by about 1900, but it continued to survive in the Northeast until the second decade of this
century (Loos, 1963:119–27, 136–41). Naturalism's influence is
unmistakable in Almeida's most famous and influential novel,
Trash (*A Bagaceira*), published in 1928, which sought to publicize
the cruel effects of the droughts that periodically devastate large
areas of the northeastern *sertão*. Almeida added yet another
scourge to thirst and starvation: The droughts were driving healthy,
free, and largely white *sertanejos* to take refuge in the immoral
world of the coastal plantations, and the traditional morality of
the backlands could not survive contact with the amoral plantation aristocracy and the "roistering band of shiftless gorillas," as
Almeida described the black descendants of slaves (1967:15).

The social histories of Gilberto Freyre also focused on the
plantation environment, but from a very different point of view.
Much of Freyre's work can be seen as an attempt to escape the
profound anxiety about miscegenation that he shared with other
white Brazilians. "Once upon a time," he wrote,

after three straight years of absence from my country, I caught sight of
a group of Brazilian seamen – mulattoes and *cafusos* – crossing
Brooklyn Bridge. . . . I know that they impressed me as being the caricatures of men, and there came to mind a phrase from a book on
Brazil written by an American traveler: "the fearfully mongrel aspect
of the population." That was the sort of thing to which miscegenation led. [1956:xxvi–xxvii]

Freyre's studies with Franz Boas at Columbia University led
him to believe that it was vital for Brazilians to separate race and
culture, "to discriminate between the effects of purely genetic
relationships and those resulting from social influences, the cultural heritage and the milieu" (1956:xxvii). In his revolutionary

history of the colonial plantation, *The Masters and the Slaves* (*Casagrande e Senzala*), first published in 1933 and the single most influential Brazilian book of the last half-century, Freyre demanded that his readers accept their nation's nonwhite heritage:

> Every Brazilian, even the light-skinned fair-haired one, carries about with him, on his soul, when not on soul and body alike – for there are many in Brazil with the mongrel mark of the *genipap* [a "dark stain on the body of children, in the inferior dorsal region, held to be a mark of mixed breeding."] – the shadow, or at least the birthmark, of the aborigine or the Negro. Along the seaboard, from Maranhão to Rio Grande do Sul, it is chiefly the Negro. The influence of the African, either direct or vague and remote.[1]

Although Freyre still described this universal physical or psychological nonwhiteness in terms of the traditional racist metaphor of the dark stain of Ham, he nonetheless insisted that it was a central, unifying element in Brazilian life and society. No region, no group, was exempt.

But what did this pervasive nonwhiteness mean; what were its implications? Freyre asserted that the nation's racial diversity was not a handicap, but a blessing: Brazilians had no need to feel themselves inferior to the inhabitants of other nations but should, in fact, recognize their own superiority. This new *ufanismo* was based upon Freyre's belief that a new and distinctive society had developed in the coastal Northeast during the colonial period, a society that was generally both more stable and more humane than its counterparts elsewhere in the Americas and one that was uniquely well adapted to its tropical environment. Moreover, the creation Freyre was later to call a "New World in the Tropics" was possible *only* because of the cultural fusion of three genetically equal races – the Portuguese, the Indian, and the African – each of which made important contributions.

This all-important cultural fusion, the foundation of the new society of colonial Brazil, was almost entirely the result of sexual interaction. Although all three races were sexually active, the most important factor in the process was the ungovernable lustfulness of Portuguese males, whom Freyre termed "unbridled

stallions" (1956:29). The massive miscegenation Freyre so carefully described was both the vehicle and the essential expression
of cultural fusion, and therefore should be viewed with pride as
the most positive element in Brazilian history and life. Those of
mixed blood were not degenerate, but superior, for they combined the cultural attitudes and physical aptitudes of the races
that formed them.

Finally, Freyre asserted, all of the negative traits associated
with Brazil's racial diversity, even the "fearfully mongrel aspect
of the population," were entirely due to defects in the physical
and social environment, and had nothing to do with genetics.
They were the temporary aftermath of the institution of slavery
itself, of coffee or sugar monoculture, of malnutrition, poorly
designed clothing, and disease – particularly the pandemic venereal diseases, the only negative consequence of the sexual
hyperactivity that made racial and cultural fusion possible (1956:71–4,
324–8). Thus, Freyre concluded, the mulattoes and *cafuzos* who
had once shamed him on the Brooklyn Bridge were not degenerate mongrels, merely sickly Brazilians.

Freyre's book and later elaborations of his basic ideas were
generally well received throughout Brazil, but they were particularly influential in the Northeast. As Thomas Skidmore has
noted, those Brazilians who wanted to believe that whiteness
had already triumphed could take Freyre's writings as entirely
historical in nature, graphic evidence that "the (primarily white)
elite had gained valuable cultural traits from their intimate contact with the African (and Indian, to a lesser extent)" in the
earlier stages of a process that was now essentially complete
(1974:192).

Ironically, however, some of the young writers of the Northeast who were most strongly influenced by Freyre produced
literary works that implicitly denied the validity of his positive
attitudes toward race and the plantation system; they returned
to themes and metaphors far more deeply embedded in Brazilian culture. Perhaps the best example of this irony is José Lins
do Rêgo (1901–57), one of the greatest novelists of the North-

east. Lins do Rêgo often said that his ideas and his novels were due entirely to Gilberto Freyre's influence (1942:116), but analysis of his most popular novel – the 1932 *Plantation Boy* (*Menino de Engenho*), perhaps the most widely read work of twentieth-century Brazilian fiction – negates those assertions.

Writing in 1936, Lins do Rêgo recalled the origins of *Plantation Boy* and the other early novels of his "Sugarcane Cycle": "The story of these books is quite a simple one. I started out merely wishing to write an autobiography which could just as well be the autobiography of any boy raised in the Big House of a Northeastern sugar plantation. What I wanted to relate was no more than a slice of life." As he wrote the deceptively simple text of *Plantation Boy*, however, he realized that he, like any writer, became "merely the instrument of forces hidden within him" (in 1966:xxvii), which caused him to move beyond both autobiography and sociology to create a new version of the central myth of Brazilian literature. The same myth, in its essence, had appeared in another deceptively simple text, Alencar's *Iracema*, and it is one that we have encountered in other texts studied in this book.

The famous last line of *Plantation Boy* – "A lost child, a plantation child" – sums up the text; it is both an elegiac account of a lost world and an etiology of personal perdition (1966:123). The first-person narrative begins when Carlos de Melo, the hero, is four years old, and his mother has just been murdered by his father. The boy is sent to the Santa Rosa plantation, the home of his maternal grandfather, where he lives for about eight years. It is as he leaves Santa Rosa, sent off to the coast and modern civilization, to a boarding school in the city, that Carlos is described, by the man he has since become, as "a lost child, a plantation child."

Santa Rosa is an old-fashioned sugar plantation. Abolition has not changed its patriarchal hierarchy of masters and servants, and its sugar is still produced using techniques developed centuries before. By the time Lins do Rêgo began to write his novel, the traditional way of life symbolized by Santa Rosa had almost disappeared, destroyed by social and economic change and by mechanization. *Plantation Boy*, at one level, is an attempt to remember and thereby to preserve a world that was being lost in time; Paulo Prado was right when he told Blaise Cendrars that Lins do Rêgo was "our Proust" (in Lins do Rêgo, 1966:xi).

Santa Rosa, however, is far more than one particular sugar plantation. It is also a refuge of natural beauty and abundance, a Brazilian Eden watched over by the godlike figure of Carlos' grandfather, who is recalled as supremely wise, kind, and just. Santa Rosa is almost destroyed twice during the course of the novel – first by flood, then by fire – but it survives these natural disasters.[2] It comes to an end, for Carlos and for us, only because he is cast out of this terrestrial paradise; it is clear that he can never return.[3] This personal perdition, which parallels the destruction of Santa Rosa by time and change, is the central focus of the text as etiology, as Carlos de Melo attempts to explain his expulsion from Eden. Throughout the novel, he tries to convince himself that his fall was the result of specific flaws in his biological and psychological makeup. Simultaneously, however, Carlos presents us with a mythic explanation that is, ultimately, far more convincing; but the context of that explanation contradicts Gilberto Freyre's positive vision of the patriarchal system and of miscegenation.

The innocent white child who first comes to Santa Rosa at the age of four is gradually, almost systematically, corrupted by that environment and by its inhabitants – above all by its black inhabitants. The narrator recalls that "we who lived in the Big House always followed the lead of the little black boys...They initiated us, through their titillating conversations about sex" (1966:56). Nor were these lessons only theoretical. Carlos, following the lead of his black playmates, first observes the "public classes in love" offered by the animals in the corral, and then practices what he has learned by copulating with cows and she-goats (1966:35). More instruction, just short of intercourse, is offered by one of the black girls, Luísa, who "initiated me, in the green springtime of my life, into the lustful practices of a hot-blooded mulatto girl. I can't even recount the things she did with me. She took me down to bathe in the river, staining my chaste innocence with her bestial concupiscence" (1966:102).

Carlos de Melo, then, is the generally melancholy prisoner of the sexuality that surrounds him on the plantation, an imprisonment symbolized by the wild birds he captures. Not even the biblical sacrifice of his pet lamb can save him from inevitable perdition. The final agent of his fall is the most depraved of the *mulatas* of Santa Rosa, Zefa Cajá; he comes of age in her arms. "I was twelve years old when I first had a woman as a man does. . .She caressed me with the voracious passion of an animal; she said that my mouth still tasted of milk, and that she wanted to gobble me up like a piece of fruit" (1966:115). It is Zefa Cajá herself who is the forbidden fruit, however: The *cajá* is the bittersweet, golden fruit of the hogplum. From her Carlos catches the venereal disease – *doença-do-mundo* (literally, "disease-of-the-world") – which prefigures his expulsion, in the next chapter, from his childhood refuge. Cast out into the larger world of the coastal city and of modern Brazil, Carlos leaves both Santa Rosa and his own innocence behind, lost beyond salvation.

José Lins do Rêgo's *Plantation Boy* falls squarely within what I believe to be the central tradition of Brazilian literature of the nineteenth and early twentieth centuries, and it can help us to define more clearly the typology of the fundamental metaphor of that tradition. That metaphor is drawn from the biblical account of Eden and of humanity's expulsion from the earthly paradise, and is based upon several fundamental ideas about the nation and its culture.

The first of these ideas is that Brazil itself is the terrestrial Eden – an image that can be traced back to Pêro Vaz de Caminha's initial reactions to the new land and its inhabitants (see S. B. de Hollanda, 1959). This Edenic vision, transformed into the *ufanista* tradition, has remained a constant in Brazilian thought for centuries and has only rarely and timorously been challenged. The enduring belief in the inexhaustible riches of the land, moreover, is still central to the elite's hopes for the future, and continues to influence policies on land use, industrialization, pollution, and energy.

The idea of the glorious and infinite goodness of the land has been coupled, almost from the beginning, with a second basic concept: the insignificance and, perhaps, even the unworthiness of the human element amid the beauty and immensity of this Eden. Writing in 1875, Melo Moraes summed up this disquiet, asserting that in "Blessed Brazil...all that is part of nature is gigantic, and only man is a pygmy" (in Sodré, 1972:150). I believe, moreover, that this image of the tiny Brazilian Adam is also linked to a third concept: that Brazil, as a nation and as a culture, is not yet fully formed, but childlike or adolescent, like Moacir, Macunaíma, or Carlos de Melo, whose "mouth still tasted of milk." This common tendency to apply the model of human development to Brazilian society and civilization can be found in writers from José de Alencar to Mário de Andrade. In the words of Octávio de Faria, a twentieth-century novelist, the nation is still "a weak, poorly educated, and impertinent child, mediocre in all things; it has a few attractive features, but its body lacks regularity and proportion; it already has vices, but does not yet have virtues" (in Sodré, 1972:56).

As important as these three ideas is the enduring preoccupation with what might be called genital history, the conviction that Brazilian history and society can only be understood as the direct result of sexual interaction between members of the national racial trinity. Miscegenation – both as the explanation for Brazil's racial and cultural diversity and as a metaphor for the formation of a distinctive national civilization – is a constant in the nation's literature and historiography, from Romantic Indianism to Modernism and the theories of Gilberto Freyre.

Miscegenation, perceived as both curse and blessing by the national elite, has a central role in the Edenic metaphor that is the focus of much of the national literature. The biblical Adam and Eve were cast out of the earthly paradise because they gave in to temptation; in the Brazilian metaphor, the sin that leads to expulsion and exile from the Edenic refuge is almost always implicit or explicit miscegenation. Racial fusion creates the nation, and as such it is often linked to the end of childhood, to an adult awareness of sexuality; but it is also the original Fall, which must be punished by exile from Eden.

Those banished from paradise because of the sin of miscegenation, however, do not move westward in search of a new, more perfect Eden always just beyond the frontier, as in the equally central geographical metaphor of North American literature. Nor do we find – except in the very different case of the overt interracial homosexuality of Adolfo Caminha's *Good Nigger* – the "two childless womanless men of opposite races," in D. H. Lawrence's phrase (1923:86), who seek harmony and goodness together in the West: Hawkeye and Chingachgook, Huck and Jim, the Lone Ranger and Tonto, and all the rest. The Brazilian Adam, alone or accompanied by his Eve, goes eastward, toward his origins – the sea, and the Portuguese identity that lies beyond it.

The Edenic metaphor – the creation or discovery of the terrestrial paradise and its destruction or loss as the result of miscegenation – was implicit, in its general outlines, in the ending of José de Alencar's *The Guarani Indian*. It became explicit, in perhaps its most influential and enduring form, in Alencar's *Iracema*. Castro Alves' *Paulo-Afonso Falls* extended the metaphor to include black Brazilians as well as Indians, and blamed expulsion from Eden on the forcible miscegenation typical of slavery; the poem's ending is a pessimistic re-creation of the last pages of *The Guarani Indian*. Moreover, the whole tradition of the stereotypical dark-skinned temptress – from Gregório de Matos' fantasies to Iracema, the "Indian Eve"; from the immoral slave girls of abolitionist arguments to Zefa Cajá and Jorge de Lima's "That Black Girl Fulô" ("Essa Negra Fulô") (1969:53–6) – can be seen as a sublimation of the white male guilt Castro Alves was trying to express. Thus it is always the dusky Eve who is seen as the primary cause of Adam's exile from Eden, and it is ironic indeed that one of the most traditional expositions of this metaphor is implicit in a poem written in 1925 by Gilberto Freyre, whose

social histories endeavored to present a far more positive view
of miscegenation:

> Plantation Boy
> No doubt about it: a plantation boy
> lived a happier life
> than a city-bred child;
> lived a carefree life, and dressed as he pleased.
>
> With his little black comrades
> he played carrousel
> on the old well-sweep:
> and the music box
> for that merry-go-round
> was the mule driver's song.
>
> He could ride a horse
> and roam the woods
> with the pickaninnies,
> and hunt *curiós*.
>
> When the cane was ripe
> there was always a farm hand
> who'd cut him a fine juicy joint to suck.
>
> He'd crouch by the millrace
> and set flies and crickets adrift in paper boats
> and pretend to himself they were pirate heroes
> in tales of adventure he'd read.
> And then one day came a naked black slave girl
> to launch the plantation boy
> on his first adventure in love.[4]
> [Freyre, 1974:193–4; translated by Barbara Shelby]

The Edenic metaphor has inevitably had a special intensity
and meaning for Brazil's great nonwhite writers, from Gonçalves
Dias to Mário de Andrade; those of mixed blood, after all, were
the products of interracial sexual contact, which that metaphor
defined as the Original Sin. Thus their fundamental sense of
alienation, like that of Gonçalves Dias' Marabá, was the inescapable result of miscegenation that had taken place in the past,
beyond their control. All sought to deny or evade that sin and its
consequences – a phenomenon that can be seen, in perhaps its

clearest form, in Mário de Andrade's insistence that the three races that formed him were not fused through miscegenation, but continued to coexist intact in the separate lozenges of his harlequinate being.

For all of these nonwhite writers, including Cruz e Sousa, the only pure black in the group, there was also a second banishment. This second, self-imposed exile was the result of their decision to be writers, to seek acceptance and success in the white world; it lay within the present rather than the past, and was their responsibility alone. Education – the assimilation of the linguistic, ideological, and cultural patterns of the white elite – was the inescapable precondition to a career in literature, but the consumption of this fruit from the tree of knowledge, and the ritualistic act of literary creation itself, separated all of these writers from their non-European racial and cultural roots.

Some nonwhites, like Machado de Assis, managed to move along the continuum to perceived whiteness; Cruz e Sousa, at the other extreme, could not escape the black prison of his appearance. But the central fact is that all, as writers, were so culturally whitened that they could never again go back to their origins: to Gonçalves Dias' Edenic childhood in Maranhão; to Machado's original, internal identity; to Cruz e Sousa's African deserts and Afro-Brazilian dancers; to Macunaíma's magic forest. All their intellectual efforts to recapture Eden – from Gonçalves Dias' obsessive studies of Indian ethnology to Mário de Andrade's equally obsessive efforts, almost a century later, to discover and describe the real, nonwhite Brazil – were doomed to futility and failure.

This second exile of the nonwhite writer, though cultural rather than genetic in origin, has nonetheless also been consistently described through the Edenic metaphor as the inevitable result of maturation and miscegenation. This miscegenation, although often presented through sexual imagery, is entirely a literary device, as metaphorical as Alencar's pairing of Ceci and Peri; it is used by nonwhite writers to symbolize the potentially destructive appeal of white culture and of whiteness itself, which has led them away from their origins and moved them along the continuum.

The earliest example of this nonwhite version of the Edenic metaphor is Gonçalves Dias' "The Indian's Song," published in 1846, eleven years before *The Guarani Indian*. The brave's passion for "the Virgin of the Christians," which leads him to betray his tribe, his religion, and his race, is a metaphor for acceptance of white, European religion and culture and for the destruction of the nonwhite Eden of the Indian world. The same theme, and almost the same image, is repeated in Cruz e Sousa's vision of the sterile and tubercular Virgin–Moon, the "Queen of Heaven," whose whiteness has an equally fatal attraction (1961:74–5, 79–80).

This nonwhite version of the Edenic metaphor, the mirror image of its white counterpart in its emphasis upon temptation and exile, is in fact the basis for all of Cruz e Sousa's powerful descriptions of a black Adam both fascinated and repulsed by the lascivious but sterile body and the serpentine hair of the white Eve – the "origin of Evil" and the physical manifestation of the destructive White Dream. It is less clearly visible in the enigmatic texts of Machado de Assis, but I believe that the same metaphor is present there as well. Machado's cautious reticence did not allow him to write openly about miscegenation, except through his allusions to two tragic North African Adams, Othello and Masinissa. Nevertheless, Eden-destroying miscegenation appears frequently in Machado's works, carefully disguised as love between individuals of different generations (in the stories of adolescent temptation, "A Woman's Arms" ["Uns Braços"] and "Midnight Mass" ["Missa do Galo"]), different social rank (Bentinho's temptation by Capitu in the childhood Eden Dom Casmurro later endeavors to reconstruct and recover), or different nationalities. Braz Cubas, for example, becomes a man at the age of seventeen – in, Machado makes certain we realize, the historically significant year of 1822, when Brazil itself became independent – as he is tempted and seduced by a European siren, Marcela. As a result of this affair, Braz is expelled from his family and from Brazil, and is sent away to Portugal. The nonwhite metaphor is inescapable, finally, in Mário de Andrade's account of Macunaíma's gradual loss of identity and potency in the modern, white world of São Paulo (a world best represented by the alien "French" whores for whose favors the hero trades the riches of the forests) and of the ultimate destruction of the culture hero and of the terrestrial paradise he was destined to explain, engender, and preserve.

Macunaíma summed up the nonwhite tradition of the Edenic metaphor; *Plantation Boy*, published four years later, is an equally detailed and comprehensive exposition of the same fundamental metaphor from the white point of view. Both these parallel, complementary traditions, moreover, are inextricably bound up with the general alienation of Brazil's great writers, the same alienation I have described as the source of what is perceived as the creative crisis of Brazilian literature as a whole during its first century of independent existence. The sadness of Olavo Bilac's three exiled races was not assuaged by independence and progress, at least not within the context of the nation's literary expression. The three sad races remained "thrice buried, thrice interred," in Cruz e Sousa's words (1961:526), within the enduring and ultimately destructive prison of the Edenic metaphor.

Notes

Introduction

1. Traces of the American genetic system of racial classification can be seen in the terms "full-blooded" and "half-breed," applied to Indians, and in the modern census categorization of Hispanic Americans by descent ("Spanish-surname Americans"), rather than by national origin or by language and culture.
2. Quite obviously, the "passing" phenomenon existed and exists in the United States as well; its basis there, however, is almost entirely somatic rather than cultural.
3. The reinterpretation of Brazilian attitudes toward race and color began, in large measure, with a presentation by a Brazilian, Oracy Nogueira (1955); the topic has since been studied by a number of Brazilian and American scholars.
4. The arbitrary and unreliable character of Brazilian census figures on race is discussed by Skidmore (1974:45).
5. José de Alencar estimated, around the middle of the nineteenth century, that only one of every thousand Brazilians reads books (in Gomes, 1958:12). The record-breaking sales of Jorge Amado's novel *Teresa Batista Cansada de Guerra* in 1973 totaled about 250,000 copies, equal to about 0.53 percent of the Brazilian population over the age of twenty at that time (Dassin, 1978:88).

1. From Indians to Indianism

1. The original makes Caminha's word play more evident: "E uma daquelas moças era toda tingida, de baixo a cima daquela tintura; e certo era tão bem feita e tão redonda, e sua vergonha (que ela não tinha) tão graciosa, que a muitas mulheres da nossa terra, vendo-lhe tais feições, fizera vergonha, por não terem a sua como ela" (Cortesão, 1967:232).

174

2. Quais são os seus doces objetos?...Prêtos
    Tem outros bens mais maciços?...Mestiços
    Quais dêstes lhe são mais gratos?...Mulatos.
    [Matos, 1969:I, 32]

3. Eu, Marília, não sou algum vaqueiro,
    Que viva de guardar alheio gado;
    De tôsco trato, de expressões grosseiro,
    Dos frios gelos e dos sóis queimado.
    Tenho próprio casal e nêle assisto;
    Dá-me vinho, legume, fruta, azeite;
    Das brancas ovelhinhas tiro a leite,
    E mais as finas lãs, de que me visto.
    Graças, Marília bela,
    Graças à minha Estrêla!
    [Gonzaga, 1972:3]

2. The songs of an exile: Antônio Gonçalves Dias

1. Eu vivo sòzinha; ninguém me procura!
    Acaso feitura
    Não sou de Tupá!
    Se algum dentre os homens de mim não se esconde:
    "Tu és," me responde,
    "Tu és Marabá!"

    .   .   .

    Meus loiros cabelos em ondas se anelam,
    O oiro mais puro tem seu fulgor;
    As brisas nos bosques de os ver se enamoram,
    De os ver tão formosos como um beija-flor!

    Mas êles respondem: "Teus longos cabelos,
    São loiros, são belos,
    Mas são anelados; tu és Marabá:
    Quero antes cabelos, bem lisos, corridos,
    Cabelos compridos,
    Não côr d'oiro fino, nem côr d'anajá."

    E as doces palavras que eu tinha cá dentro
    A quem nas direi?
    O ramo d'acácia na fronte de um homem
    Jamais cingirei:

Jamais um guerreiro da minha arasoia
Me desprenderá:
Eu vivo sòzinha, chorando mesquinha,
Que sou Marabá!

[1959: 371–2]

2. Aires da Mata Machado Filho first noted the parallels between the poem's landscape and the area around Caxias (1956), but did not develop the idea. Spix and Martius (1828:II, 815) make it clear that the word *várzea* was used in the Caxias area at that time to refer specifically to the local landscape.

3. There are more studies of the "Canção do Exílio" than of any other single Brazilian poem. This explication inevitably owes a great deal to previous critics, particularly to Bandeira (1948:133), Machado Filho (1956:9–55), Aurélio Buarque de Hollanda (1958:23–32), Cassiano Ricardo (1955:674–8), and – the most impressive of all – José Guilherme Merquior (1965:41–50).

3. The novelist as matchmaker: José de Alencar

1. Moacir is perhaps the most popular of all these names. Even American students of Portuguese are familiar with the heritage of Alencar's Indianism, for one of the characters in the dialogues Rachel de Queiroz wrote for *Modern Portuguese* (New York: Knopf, 1971), the most widely used Portuguese textbook in the United States, is named Moacir.

2. The early Brazilian novel and the problem of foreign competition are discussed by Antônio Cândido (1975:II, 109–25). Also see J. M. Vaz Pinto Coelho (1880–81) and Meyer (1973).

3. Alencar says that "Martim" means "warrior's son" in Tupi (1967:I, 260), but he also gives the Latin root (1967:I, 313).

4. The poet as slave: Antônio de Castro Alves

1. Useful sources in English for Brazilian slavery and abolitionism include Bethell (1970), Conrad (1972, 1977), and Toplin (1972).

2. The poet's parents and siblings were clearly white, judging by the family photographs preserved in the Municipal Museum in Bahia.

3.　　　　　Hoje estamos unidos a adorar-te
　　　　　Tu és a nossa glória, a nossa fé,
　　　　　Gravitar para ti é levantar-se,
　　　　　Cair-te às plantas é ficar de pé!...

. . .
Tu és tão grande como é grande o gênio
És tão brilhante como a própria luz,
Dentre os infames do calvário d'arte,
Tu fôste o Cristo, foi o palco a cruz!...
[1960:435]

4. Abram-se as ondas como virgens louras,
Para a Espôsa passar!...
"As estrêlas palpitam! – São as tochas!
Os rochedos murmuram!... – São os monges!
Reza um órgão nos céus!
Que incenso! – Os rolos que do abismo voam!
Que turíbulo enorme – Paulo Afonso!
Que sacerdote! – Deus..."
[1960:370–1]

5. "Dor, – tu és um prazer!
Grelha, – és um leito! Brasa, – és uma gema!
Cravo, – és um cetro! Chama, – um diadema
Ó morte, – és o viver!"
[1960:128]

6. Às vêzes o pastor subindo aos Alpes
Lança aos abismos a canção tremente.
Responde embaixo – o precipício enorme!
Responde em cima – o firmamento ingente!

Poeta! a voz do pegureiro errante
Em ti vibrando... se alteou!... cresceu!
Tua alma é funda – como é fundo o pego!
Teu gênio é alto – como é alto o céu!
[1960:461]

7. 'Stamos em pleno mar... Doudo no espaço
Brinca o luar – doirada borboleta –
E as vagas após êle correm... cansam
Como turba de infantes inquieta.

'Stamos em pleno mar... Do firmamento
Os astros saltam como espumas de ouro...
O mar em troca acende as ardentias
– Constelações do líquido tesouro...

'Stamos em pleno mar... Dois infinitos
Ali se estreitam num abraço insano
Azuis, dourados, plácidos, sublimes...
Qual dos dois é o céu? Qual o oceano?...

'Stamos em pleno mar... Abrindo as velas
Ao quente arfar das virações marinhas,
Veleiro brigue corre à flor dos mares
Como roçam na vaga as andorinhas...
Donde vem?... Onde vai?... Das naus errantes
Quem sabe o rumo se é tão grande o espaço?
Neste Saara os corcéis o pó levantam,
Galopam, voam, mas não deixam traço.

[1960:277]

5. A journey through the escape hatch: Joaquim Maria Machado de Assis

1. The point at which the two identities intersect is often the tip of the individual's nose. See chap. 49 of the *Memórias* (Machado, 1962:I, 563) and the stories "O Segrêdo do Bonzo" and "Idéia do Ezequiel Maya" (1962:II, 323–8, 924).
2. See, for example, "Pílades e Orestes" (1962:II, 708–15) and "Ayres e Vergueiro" (1942:II, 37–54). For doubles in Machado's works, see Sônia Brayner (1959:90–1).
3. The view that Machado had turned his back on his family and race was first and most influentially expressed in public by a very dark schoolteacher, Hemetério José dos Santos, in a letter published in the Rio de Janeiro *Gazeta de Notícias* on 29 ·November 1908, two months after Machado's death; it was reprinted, by one of Machado's friends, in the *Almanaque Brasileiro* of Garnier for 1910. There is no doubt that Santos was in error about a number of details regarding Machado's antecedents and early life, but the article is of vital importance if only as proof that other educated nonwhites in Rio de Janeiro gossiped about Machado and deeply resented his success and his passage along the continuum.

  The novelist's many admirers have almost universally damned Santos' article as a dastardly attack on the character of the great man; see, for example, Agripino Grieco (1960:197–9). I believe, however, that its basic points are entirely valid, and that Machado's works can only be understood as the product of his acute awareness of the fact that the structure of Brazilian society and his own ambition to achieve what he was capable of doing had forced him to make agonizingly difficult choices between the imperatives of the internal and external selves, between his past and his potential future. The best proof, in fact, of the novelist's essential morality, of his good character, is that he did find those choices so difficult, and endlessly debated their validity through his novels and stories.

Santos' specific charges deserve some clarification. Although Machado appears to have cut himself off from his family, as Santos asserts, it is also true that he probably was never particularly close to Maria Inês, his mulatto stepmother and the heroine of Santos' article; Machado was out on his own by the time his father married her. It is indisputable that Machado did nothing to help younger non-white writers, like Cruz e Sousa, who desperately needed his assistance. And while Magalhães Júnior (1971:117–73) has shown that the novelist worked behind the scenes to support Abolition, he clearly was never a great public champion of the cause. A most revealing example of Machado's reticence is a timid and humble letter he wrote, on 30 September 1876, to Rio Branco; the manuscript is preserved in the National Library in Rio de Janeiro. Machado's purpose was to congratulate the statesman on the fifth anniversary of the passage of the Rio Branco Law, the "Law of the Free Womb," which freed all newborn slaves; in his letter, however, Machado carefully avoided mentioning either the law's intent or its common name.

4. The interpretation of the ambiguous human text of Ezequiel is central to *Dom Casmurro*. It should also be noted that the somatic component of the racial continuum makes nonwhite parents very worried about the appearance of their children, who may be closer to the African end of the scale; the possibility of a genetic throwback to darker ancestors would certainly have preoccupied Machado and his white wife. As Counselor Aires notes in *Esau and Jacob*, "children do not always reproduce their parents" (1962:I, 981).

5. Massa notes that Machado owned two copies of the *Confessions* (1961:205–6). Machado called their author "my great Saint Augustine" in the story "Casa Velha" (1962:II, 1010).

6. For uncertainty about how well Machado really knew Italian, see Bagby (1975:227).

7. Machado's indecision about Natividade's name can be seen in his corrections and recorrections of the manuscript of *Esaú e Jacó*, preserved in the library of the Academia Brasileira de Letras. The other name Machado toyed with was Águeda, a reference to St. Agatha; the traditional iconographic representation, which shows the saint holding a tray containing her two severed breasts, would seem to have suggested to Machado both his character's maternity and the bifurcation of the two sons she bore.

8. It is possible to argue that a few of the errors and corrections in the manuscript are the result of mental slips, but that most of the emendations and remendations can again be seen as the result of Machado's indecision about the names of his characters and their symbolic value; see n. 7 to this chapter for the same phenomenon in the manuscript of *Esaú e Jacó*. In this reading, Machado first seems to have planned to call the younger woman Carmelita (perhaps symbolizing her nunlike purity as she mourns her husband's death); he also seems to have considered the name Carmo – rather than Carmelita – for the same character, which would suggest her potential maternity. He appears also to have toyed with naming the older woman Carmo (symbolizing her frustrated maternity), as he in fact finally did, but giving the younger woman the diminutive form (Carmelita) of the same name. He several times calls the older woman Fidélia, and that name would have suited her well; Aguiar's wife is the epitome of faithfulness. Machado then appears to have decided to switch, making the older woman Carmo and the younger Fidélia (symbolic of her fidelity to her husband's memory). Also, as Sayers (1968) suggests, Machado may have liked the operatic references of Tristão (Wagner) and Fidélia (Beethoven). In any case, close examination of the manuscript in the Academia Brasileira de Letras does reveal a series of careful and meticulous changes in the characters' names, using several inks and probably made at different times.

9. Machado uses the tempo and form of the entries to suggest Aires' feelings: Frequent entries mean that the old man is active, healthy, and involved; gaps suggest weakness, sorrow, or physical pain; undated entries imply psychological stress.

10. Machado wrote two stories about slavery, both published considerably after the fact of Abolition: "O Caso da Vara" and "Pai Contra Mãe" (1962:II, 577–82, 659–67). In both cases, he is interested less in the cruelty of masters to their slaves, symbolized by the curious artifacts that document slavery, than in the fact that the institution distorted society and forced utterly impossible and destructive choices – between the imperatives of the internal and external selves – upon otherwise normal and decent white Brazilians.

6. The Black Swan: João da Cruz e Sousa

1. Several Brazilian critics have explained that Cruz e Sousa's failure was all his fault; it was not the result of the racial prejudice of Brazilian society, but should be blamed on his own inability to go

along and get along, as Machado had done. See, for example, Fernando Góes (1966:63–94), who describes the poet as "a masochist."
2. There is some evidence that at least a few descendants of Cruz e Sousa may survive in poverty and obscurity. Celestino Sachet (1979:62) says that João da Cruz e Sousa Júnior left a posthumous son of his own, whose descendants live humbly in Rio de Janeiro. This claim is corroborated by the researches of Admiral Carlos da Silveira Carneiro, whose immense handwritten "Enciclopédia de Santa Catarina" is in the Biblioteca Central of the Federal University of Santa Catarina; vols. II (fol. 64) and III (fol. 62) mention great-grandchildren of the poet living in Rio de Janeiro.
3. It is hard to trace the origins of these terms, or when Cruz e Sousa's admirers began to use them, but they do appear to have been widely known among the new generation. Cruz himself spoke only of his conviction that Africa would someday produce "some new and majestic black Dante" (1961:663).

4.   Antífona
Ó Formas alvas, brancas, Formas claras
de luares, de neves, de neblinas!...
Ó Formas vagas, fluidas, cristalinas...
Incensos dos turíbulos das aras...

Formas do Amor, constelarmente puras,
de Virgens e de Santas vaporosas...
Brilhos errantes, mádidas frescuras
e dolências de lírios e de rosas...

Indefiníveis músicas supremas,
harmonias da Côr e do Perfume...
Horas do Ocaso, trêmulas, extremas,
Réquiem do Sol que a Dor da Luz resume...

Visões, salmos e cânticos serenos,
surdinas de órgãos flébeis, soluçantes...
Dormências de volúpicos venenos
sutis e suaves, mórbidos, radiantes...

Infinitos espíritos dispersos,
inefáveis, edênicos, aéreos,
fecundai o Mistério dêstes versos
com a chama ideal de todos os mistérios.

Do Sonho as mais azuis diafaneidades
que fuljam, que na Estrofe se levantem
e as emoções, tôdas as castidades
da alma do Verso, pelos versos cantem.

Que o pólen de ouro dos mais finos astros
fecunde e inflame a rima clara e ardente...
Que brilhe a correção dos alabastros
sonoramente, luminosamente.

Fôrças originais, essência, graça
de carnes de mulher, delicadezas...
Todo êsse eflúvio que por ondas passa
do Éter nas róseas e áureas correntezas...

Cristais diluídos de clarões alacres,
desejos, vibrações, ânsias, alentos,
fulvas vitórias, triunfamentos acres,
os mais estranhos estremecimentos...

Flôres negras do tédio e flôres vagas
de amôres vãos, tantálicos, doentios...
Fundas vermelhidões de velhas chagas
em sangue, abertas, escorrendo em rios...

Tudo! vivo e nervoso e quente e forte,
nos turbilhões quiméricos do Sonho,
passe, cantando, ante o perfil medonho
e o tropel cabalístico da Morte...

　　　　　　　　　　　　　　　　[1961:69–70]

5.　　　　　　　　　　Lésbia
Cróton selvagem, tinhorão lascivo,
planta mortal, carnívora, sangrenta,
da tua carne báquica rebenta
a vermelha explosão de um sangue vivo.

Nesse lábio mordente e convulsivo,
ri, ri risadas de expressão violenta
o Amor, trágico e triste, e passa, lenta,
a morte, o espasmo gélido, aflitivo...

Lésbia nervosa, fascinante e doente,
cruel e demoníaca serpente
das flamejantes atrações do gôzo.

Dos teus seios acídulos, amargos,
fluem capros aromas e os letargos,
os ópios de um luar tuberculoso...

　　　　　　　　　　　　　　　　[1961:70–1]

6. Baudelaire's influence is clear; see his "La chevelure," "Le serpent qui danse," and "*Sed non satiata*" in the *Fleurs du mal*. Cruz e Sousa dedicated one of the *Evocações*, "No Inferno," to Baudelaire (1961: 580–4).

7.   Lubricidade
Quisera ser a serpe venenosa
que dá-te mêdo e dá-te pesadelos
para envolver-me, ó Flor maravilhosa,
nos flavos turbilhões dos teus cabelos.

Quisera ser a serpe veludosa
para, enroscada em múltiplos novelos,
saltar-te aos seios de fluidez cheirosa
e babujá-los e depois mordê-los...

Talvez que o sangue impuro e flamejante
do teu lânguido corpo de bacante,
da langue ondulação de águas do Reno

Estranhamente se purificasse...
Pois que um veneno de áspide voraz
deve ser morto com igual veneno...
                                     [1961:72]

8. See Luís Gama's famous poem "Quem Sou Eu" (1944:97–100).

9.   Acrobata da Dor
Gargalha, ri, num riso de tormenta,
como um palhaço, que desengonçado,
nervoso, ri, num riso absurdo, inflado
de uma ironia e de uma dor violenta.

Da gargalhada atroz, sanguinolenta,
agita os guizos, e convulsionado
Salta, gavroche, salta *clown*, varado
pelo estertor dessa agonia lenta...

Pedem-te bis e um bis não se despreza!
Vamos! reteza os músculos, reteza
nessas macabras piruêtas d'aço...

E embora caias sôbre o chão, fremente,
afogado em teu sangue estuoso e quente,
ri! Coração, tristíssimo palhaço.
                                     [1961:92]

Also see the essay "Psicose" (1961:710–11) and Cruz e Sousa's frequent references to Gwynplaine, the hero of Hugo's novel *L'Homme
qui rit* (1869) and one of Cruz e Sousa's most important symbols.
Gwynplaine is of noble birth, but is captured and surgically deformed by his captors so that he may be sold as a clown; his face
always appears to be laughing.

10. Cruz e Sousa could never entirely escape Haeckel's hated influence. The term "Nubian," which the poet here applies to Gavita and which Vítor used to describe Cruz e Sousa, was reserved by Haeckel for a slightly superior species of *ulotrichi* (1876:II, 320–1).

11.   Sexta-feira Santa
Lua absíntica, verde, feiticeira,
pasmada como um vício monstruoso...
Um cão estranho fuça na esterqueira,
univando para o espaço fabuloso.

É esta a negra e santa Sexta-feira!
Cristo está morto, como um vil leproso,
chagado e frio, na feroz cegueira
da Morte, o sangue roxo e tenebroso.

A serpente do mal e do pecado
um sinistro veneno esverdeado
verte do Morto na mudez serena.

Mas da sagrada Redenção do Cristo
em vez do grande Amor, puro, imprevisto,
brotam fosforescências de gangrena!
                                [1961:212–13]

12.   Ódio Sagrado
Ó meu ódio, meu ódio majestoso,
meu ódio santo e puro e benfazejo,
unge-me a fronte com teu grande beijo,
torna-me humilde e torna-me orgulhoso.

Humilde, com os humildes generoso,
orgulhoso com os sêres sem Desejo,
sem Bondade, sem Fé e sem lampejo
de sol fecundador e carinhoso.

Ó meu ódio, meu lábaro bendito,
de minh'alma agitado no infinito,
através de outros lábaros sagrados,

ódio são, ódio bom! sê meu escudo
contra os vilões do Amor, que infamam tudo
das sete tôrres dos mortais Pecados!
                                [1961:205]

7. From despair to Modernism

1. The most complete souce on Brazilian ideas about race during this period is Thomas E. Skidmore's brilliant study (1974).

2. Because Oswald de Andrade and Mário de Andrade, though not related, share the same family name, Brazilian critics generally refer to them by their given names; I have followed this convention here.

8. The harlequin: Mário de Andrade

1. See note 2 to the preceding chapter for references to Oswald de Andrade and Mário de Andrade by their given names. For Mário's extraliterary activities ad a musicologist, art historian, and public servant, see Coli Júnior (1972), Dassin (1978), and Duarte (1971).
2. See N. N. Coelho (1970), Feres (1969), Grembecki (1969), L. C. Lima (1968:33–132), Lopez (1969, 1972, 1974), and Proença (1977).
3. 　　　　　Eu sou um escritor difícil,
　　　　　Porém culpa de quem é...
　　　　　Todo difícil é fácil,
　　　　　Abasta a gente saber.
　　　　　　　　　　[1972d:243]
4. The figure of the harlequin – and, more generally, of the clown – was part of what Mário described as the universal "waters of modernity" in which he moved (1966:24). Mário, however, took a symbol that was commonly used in European and Brazilian literature and art of the period and made it his own, as a representation of racial diversity.
5. 　　　　　As primaveras de sarcasmo
　　　　　intermitentemente no meu coração arlequinal...
　　　　　Intermitentemente...
　　　　　Outras vezes é um doente, um frio
　　　　　na minha alma doente como um longo som redondo...
　　　　　　　　　　[1968a:22]
6. 　　　　　Mas...olhai, oh meus olhos saudosos dos ontens
　　　　　êsse espetáculo encantado da Avenida!
　　　　　Revivei, oh gaúchos paulistas ancestremente!
　　　　　e oh cavalos de cólera sanguínea!
　　　　　Laranja da China, laranja da China, laranja da China!
　　　　　Abacate, cambucá e tangerina!
　　　　　Guardate! Aos aplausos do esfusiante clown,
　　　　　heroico sucessor da raça heril dos bandeirantes,
　　　　　passa galhardo um filho de imigrante,
　　　　　loiramente domando um automóvel!
　　　　　　　　　　[1968a:46]
7. The term "code" is used by Haroldo de Campos (1973:266–74) in a considerably more restricted sense; I have expanded this useful concept.

8. My analysis does not cover all the codes that appear in Mário's text; worthy of more detailed study are those focused upon plants, animals, and monsters. I have, in general, avoided references to Mário's sources for the incidents described; readers are directed to Lopez (1974) and Proença (1977).

9. The manuscript of the chapter titles for an early version of *Macunaíma* shows that the original name of the chapter that describes the parrot's survival and departure was "Eiffel Tower" (Campos, 1973:289, 303). Campos suggests a link with Mallarmé; my own guess would be that Mário originally planned to have the bird repeat one of Santos-Dumont's most famous aeronautical feats, a flight around the Eiffel Tower.

10. The reference is to the very prominent crop of this species. From a distance, the king vulture appears to have two heads, one above the other.

11. This section was considerably longer and more explicit in the first two editions, but Mário cut it for the third. The suppressed sections are in Proença (1977:42–43).

12. Proença (1977:236) notes a true case, cited by Humboldt, of a parrot who was the only source for the language of a vanished tribe.

13. Mario described José de Alencar as a "Father-of-the-Living [a *Pódole*] who shines in the vast fields of the sky" (in Lopez, 1974:75). He also wrote that to "go be a star...is the ultimate destiny of beings...with nothing left to do on this earth" (1966:218). Mário's suggestion that he shared this destiny himself appears in a letter of 16 July 1930 (1968b:15–16).

Conclusion: The Edenic metaphor

1. Freyre, 1956:278. The note in brackets is by the translator, Samuel Putnam, citing Hildebrando Lima and Gustavo Barroso's definition of the word *jenipapo*.

2. Interestingly enough, precisely the same basic metaphoric framework had already appeared, independently, in Manuel Bandeira's poem, "Evocação do Recife," written in 1925 (Bandeira, 1958:I, 198–200). Bandeira's elegiac evocation of the Recife of his childhood includes first fire and then flood; these disasters and the more general theme of the final loss of this refuge of simplicity and goodness are inextricably linked to the poet's first sexual experiences.

3. What happens to those who seek to return to Eden is exemplified, in *Menino de Engenho*, by the figure of Tio Juca – both powerless and depraved. Carlos de Melo's own attempt to go back to Santa Rosa is

described in a later novel in the "Sugarcane Cycle," *Bangüê,* published in 1934, but that attempt too is a total failure.

4. Menino de Engenho
O menino de engenho era decerto
criatura menos sacrificada à gravidade
de trajo e vida que o nascido nas cidades.

Nas almanjarras,
com os muleques
seus camaradas
leva-pancadas
brincava de carrossel
um carrossel
a que servia
de caixa de música
e cantiga do tangedor.

Montava a cavalo
saía pelo mato
com o muleque
a pegar curiós.

No tempo de cana madura
chupava com delícia os rolêtes
que lhe torneavam a faca
os negros do engenho.

Gostava de fazer navegar
na água das levadas
em navios de papel
môscas e grilos
personagens dos romances de aventura
que inventava
antes de conhecer negras nuas
e viver seus primeiros romances de amor.

[Freyre, 1971:129–30]

Selected bibliography

This list is confined to works directly referred to in the text. It is not intended as a full or systematic bibliography of Brazilian literature.

Agassiz, Elizabeth C., and Agassiz, Louis. 1886. *A Journey in Brazil*. Boston: Houghton Mifflin.

Alencar, Heron de. 1956. José de Alencar e a ficção romântica. In *A Literatura no Brasil*, ed. Afrânio Coutinho, vol. I, pt. 2, pp. 837–948. Rio de Janeiro: Sul Americana.

Alencar, José de. 1886. *Iraçéma the Honey-Lips*, trans. Isabel Burton. London: Bickers and Sons.

1960. *Obra Completa*, vol. IV. Rio de Janeiro: Aguilar.

1967. *Romances Ilustrados*, 6th ed., 7 vols. Rio de Janeiro: Olympio.

Almeida, Guilherme de. 1952. *Tôda a Poesia*, vol. IV. São Paulo: Martins.

Almeida, José Américo de. 1967. *A Bagaceira*, 9th ed. rev. Rio de Janeiro: Olympio.

Alves, Henrique L. 1973. *Mário de Andrade*. São Paulo: Ed. do Escritor.

Andrade, Mário de. 1961. *Poesia*, ed. Dantas Motta. Rio de Janeiro: AGIR.

1966. *Cartas a Manuel Bandeira*. Rio de Janeiro: Ed. de Ouro.

1968a. *Hallucinated City*, trans. Jack E. Tomlins. Nashville, Tenn.: Vanderbilt University Press.

1968b. *Mário de Andrade Escreve Cartas*, ed. Lygia Fernandes. Rio de Janeiro: Ed. do Autor.

1972a. *Aspectos da Literatura Brasileira*, 4th ed. São Paulo: Martins.

1972b. *Macunaíma*, 7th ed. São Paulo: Martins.

1972c. *Obra Imatura*, 2nd ed. São Paulo: Martins.

1972d. *Poesias Completas*, 3rd ed. São Paulo: Martins.

Andrade, Oswald de. 1967. *Trechos Escolhidos*, ed. Haroldo de Campos. Rio de Janeiro: AGIR.

Araripe Júnior, Tristão de A. 1963. *Obra Crítica*, vol. III. Rio de Janeiro: M.E.C.

Azevedo, Aluísio. 1965. *Casa de Pensão*. São Paulo: Martins.
Azevedo, Artur. n.d. *Contos Efémeros*, 2nd ed. Rio de Janeiro: Garnier.
Azevedo, Fernando de. 1950. *Brazilian Culture*, trans. W. R. Crawford. New York: Macmillan.
Bader, Clarisse. 1877. *La femme romaine*. Paris: Didier.
Bagby, A. I. 1975. Machado de Assis and foreign languages. *Luso-Brazilian Review*, 12(2): 225–33.
Bandeira, Manuel. 1948. A poética de Gonçalves Dias. In *Gonçalves Dias: Conferências*, pp. 111–37. Rio de Janeiro: Academia Brasileira de Letras.
1958. *Poesia e Prosa*, 2 vols. Rio de Janeiro: Aguilar.
Bastide, Roger. 1943. *A Poesia Afro-Brasileira*. São Paulo: Martins.
Basto Cordeiro, Francisca de. 1961. *Machado de Assis que Eu Vi*. Rio de Janeiro: São José.
Bastista, M. R.; Lopez, Telê Porto Ancona; and Soares de Lima, Yone (eds.). 1972. *Brasil: Primeiro Tempo Modernista – 1917/29*. São Paulo: Instituto de Estudos Brasileiros.
Baudelaire, Charles. 1923. *Curiosités esthétiques*, ed. Jacques Crépet. Paris: L. Conard.
Bethell, Leslie. 1970. *The Abolition of the Brazilian Slave Trade*. Cambridge: Cambridge University Press.
Bilac, Olavo. 1964. *Poesias*, 28th ed. Rio de Janeiro: Alves.
Boxer, C. R. 1962. *The Golden Age of Brazil*. Berkeley: University of California Press.
Brayner, Sônia. 1979. *Labirinto do Espaço Romanesco*. Rio de Janeiro: Civilização Brasileira.
Broca, José Brito. 1960. *A Vida Literária no Brasil – 1900*, 2nd ed. Rio de Janeiro: Olympio.
Burns, E. Bradford. 1968. *Nationalism in Brazil*. New York: Praeger.
Caldwell, Helen. 1960. *The Brazilian Othello of Machado de Assis*. Berkeley: University of California Press.
1970. *Machado de Assis*. Berkeley: University of California Press.
Calmon, Pedro. 1940. *História Social do Brasil*, 2nd ed., vol. II. São Paulo: C.E.N.
1973. *Castro Alves: O Homem e a Obra*. Rio de Janeiro: Olympio.
Calógeras, João Pandiá. 1939. *A History of Brazil*, trans. and ed. P. A. Martin. Chapel Hill: University of North Carolina Press.
Câmara, Eugênia. 1864. *Segredos d'Alma*. Fortaleza: Tipografia Constitucional.
Caminha, Adolfo. 1966. *Bom-Crioulo*. Rio de Janeiro: Ed. de Ouro.
Campos, Haroldo de. 1973. *Morfologia do Macunaíma*. São Paulo: Perspectiva.
Cândido, Antônio. 1970. *Vários Escritos*. São Paulo: Duas Cidades.

1975. *Formação da Literatura Brasileira*, 5th ed., 2 vols. São Paulo: Universidade de São Paulo.

Carneiro, Carlos da Silveira. n.d. Enciclopédia de Santa Catarina, manuscript in the library of the Federal University of Santa Catarina, Florianópolis.

Castello, José Aderaldo (ed.). 1953. *A Polêmica sôbre "A Confederação dos Tamoios."* São Paulo: Universidade de São Paulo.

Castro Alves, Antônio de. 1921. *Obras Completas*, ed. Afrânio Peixoto, 2 vols. Rio de Janeiro: Alves.

1960. *Obra Completa*, ed. Eugênio Gomes. Rio de Janeiro: Aguilar.

Celso, Afonso. 1901. *Porque Me Ufano do Meu País*. Rio de Janeiro: Laemmert.

Centenário de Cruz e Sousa: Interpretações. 1962. Florianópolis: Comissão Oficial de Festejos.

Chasin, J. 1978. *O Integralismo de Plínio Salgado*. São Paulo: Ciências Humanas.

Cidade, Hernani (ed.). 1940. *Padre António Viera*, 4 vols. Lisbon: Agência Geral das Colónias.

Codman, J. 1870. *Ten Months in Brazil*. Edinburgh: R. Grant.

Coelho, J. M. Vaz Pinto. 1880–1. Da propriedade literária no Brasil. *Revista Brasileira*, 6: 474–91, 8: 474–98.

Coelho, Nelly Novaes. 1970. *Mário de Andrade para a Jovem Geração*. São Paulo: Saraiva.

Coli Júnior, J. S. 1972. Mário de Andrade: Introdução ao pensamento musical. *Revista do Instituto de Estudos Brasileiros*, 12: 111–36.

Conrad, R. 1972. *The Destruction of Brazilian Slavery, 1850–1888*. Berkeley: University of California Press.

1977. *Brazilian Slavery: An Annotated Research Bibliography*. Boston: G.K. Hall.

Cortesão, J. (ed.). 1967. *A Carta de Pêro Vaz de Caminha*. Lisbon: Portugália.

Coutinho, A. (ed.). 1979. *Cruz e Sousa: Fortuna Crítica*. Rio de Janeiro: Civilização Brasileira.

Cruz e Sousa, João da. 1923–4. *Obras Completas*, 2 vols. Rio de Janeiro: Anuário do Brasil.

1961. *Obra Completa*, ed. Andrade Muricy. Rio de Janeiro: Aguilar.

Cunha, Euclides da. 1944. *Rebellion in the Backlands*, trans. Samuel Putnam. Chicago: University of Chicago Press.

Cunha, Fausto. 1971. *O Romantismo no Brasil*. Rio de Janeiro: Paz e Terra.

Dassin, J. R. 1978. *Política e Poesia em Mário de Andrade*. São Paulo: Duas Cidades.

David, Carlos (ed.). 1957. Centenário de José Veríssimo. *Revista do Livro*, ano 2(5): 147–80.

Degler, C. N. 1971. *Neither Black nor White*. New York: Macmillan.
Duarte, P. 1971. *Mário de Andrade por Êle Mesmo*. São Paulo: Edart.
Faoro, R. 1974. *Machado de Assis: A Pirâmide e o Trapézio*. São Paulo: C.E.N.
Feres, N. T. 1969. *Leituras em Francês de Mário de Andrade*. São Paulo: Instituto de Estudos Brasileiros.
Finnegan, R. 1977. *Oral Poetry*. Cambridge: Cambridge University Press.
Freitas Júnior, Otávio de. 1941. *Ensaios de Crítica de Poesia*. Recife: Imprensa Industrial.
Freyre, G. 1956. *The Masters and the Slaves*, trans. Samuel Putnam, 2nd ed. rev. New York: Knopf.
1971. *Seleta para Jovens*. Rio de Janeiro: Olympio.
1974. *The Gilberto Freyre Reader*, trans. Barbara Shelby. New York: Knopf.
Gama, L. 1944. *Trovas Burlescas e Escritos em Prosa*, ed. F. Góes. São Paulo: Cultura.
Góes, F. 1966. *O Espelho Infiel*. São Paulo: Conselho Estadual de Cultura.
Gomes, E. 1953. *Prata de Casa*. Rio de Janeiro: A Noite.
1958. *Aspectos do Romance Brasileiro*. Bahia: Progresso.
Gonçalves de Magalhães, D. J. 1865. *Suspiros Poéticos e Saudades*, 3rd ed. Rio de Janeiro: Garnier.
Gonçalves Dias, Antônio. 1909. *Meditação*. Rio de Janeiro: Garnier.
1910. *O Brasil e a Oceânia*, 2nd ed. Rio de Janeiro: Garnier.
1959. *Poesia Completa e Prosa Escolhida*. Rio de Janeiro: Aguilar.
Gonzaga, T. A. 1972. *Marília de Dirceu*. São Paulo: Martins.
Graça Aranha, J. Pereira da. 1969. *Obra Completa*. Rio de Janeiro: I.N.L.
Grembecki, M. H. 1969. *Mário de Andrade e "L'Esprit Nouveau."* São Paulo: Instituto de Estudos Brasileiros.
Grieco, Agripino. n.d.. *Evolução da Poesia Brasileira*, 2nd ed. Rio de Janeiro: H. Antunes.
1960. *Machado de Assis*, 2nd ed. rev. Rio de Janeiro: Conquista.
Haberly, D. T. 1972. Abolitionism in Brazil: Anti-slavery and anti-slave. *Luso-Brazilian Review*, 9(2): 30–46.
1975. Eugênia Câmara: The life and verse of an actress. *Luso-Brazilian Review*, 12(2): 162–74.
Haddad, J. A. 1953. *Revisão de Castro Alves*, 3 vols. São Paulo: Saraiva.
Haeckel, E. 1876. *The History of Creation*, trans. E. R. Lankester, 2 vols. New York: Appleton.
Hollanda, Aurélio Buarque de. 1958. *Território Lírico*. Rio de Janeiro: O Cruzeiro.
Hollanda, Sérgio Buarque de. 1959. *Visão do Paraíso: Os Motivos Edênicos no Descobrimento e Colonização do Brasil*. Rio de Janeiro: Olympio.

Jorge, F. 1957. Aspectos inéditos de Cruz e Sousa. *Revista Brasiliense, no.* 11: 129–34.

Keyserling, H. A., Graf von. 1927. *The World in the Making,* trans. M. Samuel. New York: Harcourt Brace.

Koch-Grünberg, T. 1924. *Vom Roroima zum Orinoco: Ergebnisse einer Reise in Nord-brasilien und Venezuela in den Jahren 1911–13,* vol. II. Stuttgart: Strecker und Schröder.

Lawrence, D. H. 1923. *Studies in Classic American Literature.* New York: T. Seltzer.

Leal, A. H. 1874. *Antônio Gonçalves Dias.* Lisbon: Imprensa Nacional.

Leitão de Barros, José J. M. 1949. *Como Eu Vi Castro Alves e Eugênia Câmara no Vendaval Maravilhoso de Suas Vidas.* Lisbon: Livros de Portugal.

Ley, C. D. (ed. and trans.). 1947. *Portuguese Voyages, 1498–1663.* London: Dent.

Lima, Alceu Amoroso. 1966. *Estudos Literários,* vol. I. Rio de Janeiro: Aguilar.

Lima, Jorge de. 1969. *Antologia Poética.* Rio de Janeiro: Sabiá.

Lima, L. C. 1968. *Lira e Antilira.* Rio de Janeiro: Civilização Brasileira.

Lins do Rêgo, José. *Gordos e Magros.* Rio de Janeiro: Casa do Estudante do Brasil.

    1966. *Menino de Engenho,* ed. J. A. Castello, 10th ed. Rio de Janeiro: Olympio.

Loos, D. S. 1963. *The Naturalistic Novel of Brazil.* New York: The Hispanic Institute.

Lopez, Telê Porto Ancona. 1969. Cronologia geral da obra de Mário de Andrade. *Revista do Instituto de Estudos Brasileiros,* 7: 139–72.

    1972. *Mário de Andrade: Ramais e Caminho.* São Paulo: Duas Cidades.

    1974. *Macunaíma: A Margem e o Texto.* São Paulo: HUCITEC.

Mac Adam, Alfred J. 1972. Rereading *Ressurreição. Luso-Brazilian Review,* 9(2): 47–57.

Macedo, Joaquim Manuel de. n.d. *As Vítimas-Algozes: Quadros da Escravidão,* 2nd ed., 2 vols. Rio de Janeiro: Garnier.

Machado de Assis, J. M. 1942. *Contos Fluminenses,* vol. II. Rio de Janeiro: Jackson.

    1962. *Obra Completa,* ed. A. Coutinho, 3 vols. Rio de Janeiro: Aguilar.

Machado Filho, Aires da Mata. 1956. *Crítica de Estilos.* Rio de Janeiro: AGIR.

Magalhães Júnior, R. 1971. *Machado de Assis Desconhecido,* 4th ed. rev. São Paulo: LISA.

    1975. *Poesia e Vida de Cruz e Sousa,* 3rd ed. rev. Rio de Janeiro: Civilização Brasileira.

Malinoff J. 1976. From anguish to affirmation: A study of Afro-Brazilian poetry. Ph.D. dissertation, Harvard University.

Martins, Wilson. 1969. *O Modernismo*, 3rd ed. rev. São Paulo: Cultrix.

Martins Moreira, Thiers. 1970. *Visão em Vários Tempos*, vol. I. Rio de Janeiro: São José.

Massa, Jean-Michel. 1961. La bibliothèque de Machado de Assis. *Revista do Livro, ano VI*(21–2): 195–238.

1971. *A Juventude de Machado de Assis*, trans. M. A. de Moura Matos. Rio de Janeiro: Civilização Brasileira.

Matos, Gregório de. 1969. *Crônica do Viver Baiano Seiscentista*, ed. James Amado, 7 vols. Bahia: Janaína.

Meireles, Mário M. 1960. *História do Maranhão*. Rio de Janeiro: D.A.S.P.

Melo Franco, Afonso Arinos de. 1937. *O Índio Brasileiro e a Revolução Francesa*. Rio de Janeiro: Olympio.

Menezes, Raimundo de. 1965. *José de Alencar*. São Paulo: Martins.

Merquior, J. G. 1965. *Razão do Poema*. Rio de Janeiro: Civilização Brasileira.

Meyer, M. 1973. O que é, ou quem foi Sinclair das Ilhas? *Revista do Instituto de Estudos Brasileiros, 14*: 40–50.

Miguel-Pereira, L. 1943. *A Vida de Gonçalves Dias*. Rio de Janeiro: Olympio.

Nogueira, Oracy. 1955. Preconceito racial de marca e preconceito racial de origem. In *Anais do XXXI Congresso Internacional de Americanistas*, ed. H. Baldus, vol. I, pp. 409–34. São Paulo: Anhembi.

Orico, O. 1977. *José de Alencar*, 2nd ed. rev. Rio de Janeiro: Cátedra.

Pauli, E. n.d. *Cruz e Sousa*. São Paulo: Ed. do Escritor.

Pedro II (Pedro de Alcântara). 1898. *Sonetos do Exílio*. Paris: n.p.

Peixoto, Afrânio. 1931. *Noções de História da Literatura Brasileira*. Rio de Janeiro: Alves.

1976. *Castro Alves: O Poeta e o Poema*, 5th ed. São Paulo: C.E.N.

Peres, F. da Rocha. 1967. Negros e mulatos em Gregório de Matos. *Afro-Ásia*, nos. 4–5: 59–75.

Pike, F. B. (ed.). 1969. *Latin American History: Select Problems*. New York: Harcourt, Brace and World.

Pinheiro Machado, G. 1976. *A Filosofia no Brasil*, 3rd ed. São Paulo: Cortez e Moraes.

Prado, Paulo. 1944. *Retrato do Brasil*, 5th ed. São Paulo: Brasiliense.

Proença, M. Cavalcanti. 1971. *Estudos Literários*, ed. A. Houaiss. Rio de Janeiro: Olympio.

1972. *José de Alencar na Literatura Brasileira*, 2nd ed. Rio de Janeiro: Civilização Brasileira.

1977. *Roteiro de Macunaíma*, 4th ed. Rio de Janeiro: Civilização Brasileira.

Quieroz Júnior, T. 1975. *Preconceito de Côr e a Mulata na Literatura Brasileira*. São Paulo: Ática.

Revista do Livro. 1958. Edição comemorativa do cinqüentenário da morte de Machado de Assis. *Ano 3(11).*

Ricardo, Cassiano. 1955. Gonçalves Dias e o indianismo. In *A Literatura no Brasil,* ed. Afrânio Coutinho, vol. I, pt. 2, pp. 659–742. Rio de Janeiro: Sul Americana.

1957. *Poesias Completas.* Rio de Janeiro: Olympio.

Rodríguez Monegal, E. 1977. Anacronismos: Mário de Andrade y Guimarães Rosa en el contexto de la novela hispanoamericana. *Revista Iberoamericana,* 43(98–9): 109–15.

Romero, Sílvio. 1960. *História da Literatura Brasileira,* 6th ed. Rio de Janeiro: Olympio.

Romero, Sílvio, and Ribeiro, João. 1909. *Compêndio de História da Literatura Brasileira,* 2nd ed. rev. Rio de Janeiro: Alves.

Roquette-Pinto, E. 1948. Gonçalves Dias e os índios. In *Gonçalves Dias: Conferências,* pp. 83–93. Rio de Janeiro: Academia Brasileira de Letras.

Sachet, C. 1979. *A Literatura de Santa Catarina.* Florianópolis: Lunardelli.

Saunders, J. 1972. Class, color, and prejudice: A Brazilian counterpoint. In *Racial Tensions and National Identity,* ed. E. Q. Campbell, pp. 141–65. Nashville, Tenn.: Vanderbilt University Press.

Sayers, R. S. 1956. *The Negro in Brazilian Literature.* New York: The Hispanic Institute.

1968. A caminho de Bayreuth: A Música na obra de Machado de Assis. *Revista Hispánica Moderna, ano* 34(3–4): 776–90.

Schaden, E., and Pereira, J.B.B. 1969. Exploração antropológica. In *História Geral da Civilização Brasileira,* ed. S. B. de Hollanda, 2nd ed., vol. II, pt. 3, pp. 426–44. São Paulo: Difusão Européia do Livro.

Schopenhauer, A. 1958. *The World as Will and Representation,* trans. E. F.J. Payne, 2 vols. Indian Hills, Colo.: Falcon's Wing Press.

Silva Brito, Mário de. 1971. *História do Modernismo Brasileiro,* 3rd ed., vol. I. Rio de Janeiro: Civilização Brasileira.

Skidmore, T. E. 1974. *Black into White: Race and Nationality in Brazilian Thought.* New York: Oxford University Press.

Smith, T. Lynn. 1963. *Brazil: People and Institutions.* Baton Rouge: Louisiana State University Press.

Sodré, Hélio. 1972. *Brasil: Uma Civilização.* Rio de Janeiro: Ed. Rio.

Spix, J. B. von, and Martius, C.F.P. von. 1828. *Reise in Brasilien,* vol. II. Munich: Lentner.

Tolman, Jon M. 1975. Castro Alves, poeta amoroso. *Luso-Brazilian Review,* 12(2): 241–62.

Toplin, R. B. 1972. *The Abolition of Slavery in Brazil.* New York: Atheneum.

Varnhagen, Francisco Adolfo de. 1841. Memória sôbre a necessidade do estudo e ensino das línguas indígenas do Brasil. *Revista do Instituto Histórico e Geográfico Brasileiro*, 3: 53–63.

Veríssimo, José. 1976. *Estudos de Literatura Brasileira*, 1st ser. Belo Horizonte: Itatiaia.

Véron, E. 1879. *Aesthetics*, trans. W. H. Armstrong. London: Chapman & Hall.

Vítor, Nestor. 1969. *Obra Crítica*, vol. I. Rio de Janeiro: M.E.C.

Index